Under the Shadow
of
Meon Hill

The Lower Quinton & Hagley Wood Murders

PAUL NEWMAN

Abraxas & DGR Books

ACKNOWLEDGEMENTS

This reappraisal of an old crime was enabled by notes taken by Tess Kingham from the autopsy, witness interviews and special reports [5/4/45 & 30/4/45] of the original investigation conducted by Inspector Fabian of Scotland Yard and passed on to the Warwickshire Constabulary; also Tess's copies of letters and articles by Cecil Williamson. The Coroner's Report was also a fascinating primary source, for which I thank Warwickshire County Record Office who provided me a copy. Fabian's memoirs *Fabian of the Yard* (1955) and *Anatomy of Crime* (1970) were useful reference points for the popular market, but the latter does contain a confusing aerial photograph for, geographically speaking, the crime might be relocated as the 'Upper Quinton Murder'.

Donald McCormick's *Murder by Witchcraft* was an engrossing narrative, though (see chapter *Murder by Witchcraft, p. 96*) 'over creative' in its employment of source material. David Taylor's lively article in *Paranormal* on The Hagley Wood Murder was absorbing and Joyce Coley's more detailed *Bella* a fine example of reflective research and local history. I should also add that meeting them both, and sharing their generous exchange of views, greatly enhanced the creation of this book. Similarly Michael Howard, an expert on paganism, looked over the text and came out with a number of wise suggestions and emendations, nearly all of which I have incorporated. Once again, I must thank my friend Lee Cooper for overhauling this book and checking the proofs.

CONTENTS –

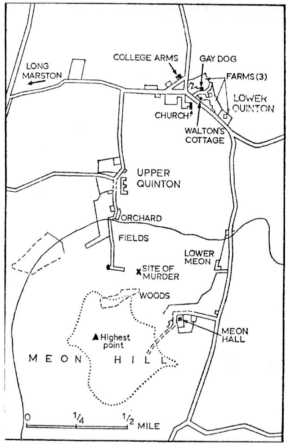

(Above) Hillground where Charles Walton was killed.
(Below) Map of Lower Quinton showing murder site.

INTRODUCTION

Nearly ten years ago, when working on a book called *The Tregerthen Horror,* I came to a point where I was obliged to find out the names of a group of occultists who were active in Cornwall in 1938 and peripherally involved in the death of Ka Cox – ex-sweetheart of the poet Rupert Brooke – at a lonely, haunted cottage on Zennor Carn. The trail petered out. Few people had a living memory of the incident – even a search of Home Office files offered nothing.

Several of my enquiries were blocked by the Data Protection Act, barring the release of sensitive information for fear of upsetting or damaging the reputation of the living relatives of those concerned. Then there was the added problem of files destroyed or lost through accident, fire or transference to another building or archive. Police records are especially difficult to access because they are not open to casual evaluation by any researcher who, more often than not, will be told to seek the information through newspapers or public sources.

In the course of my researches, I phoned the Witchcraft Museum at Boscastle – an enquiry concerning the late Cecil Williamson. I was given the name Tess Kingham who, I understood, was looking into the rather unusual brew of occultism and espionage activities that took place during World War Two. Rather brashly, I phoned Tess who told me that for several years she had been fitfully investigating a group of people in connection with the notorious 'Walton' or Lower Quinton Murder. I was glad she had a fairly comical, chatty attitude towards sharing her information. While examining the Warwickshire Police files, she had found a document relating to my area of enquiry, naming those involved and their background. Kindly she made available the information which turned out not only to clarify the incident but broaden and deepen its perspective.

So far as Tess was concerned, researching murders of bygone eras was a hobby. A mild online curiosity on my part revealed she had a more dashing social profile than I anticipated. From 1997 – 2001, she was MP for Gloucester, being elected as one of the 101 Labour women MPs in 1997. She took her place on the House of Commons Select

Committee for International Development and Strategic Exports (Arms controls). While in Parliament, she saw through improvements to UK fire safety legislation and, backed by the Cystic Fibrosis Trust, lobbied Government for a national CF screening programme for babies. Finally she walked out on politics disillusioned. Initially she had looked forward to the prospect of being at the centre of debate with the opportunity for vetting and modifying legislation but "what I got instead," she gloomily reflected, "was days and nights watching opposition MPs such as Eric Forth and his sad friends endlessly thrusting their groins around the Chamber in mock combat with Labour ministers – achieving absolutely nothing."

Among the glorious repertoire were tactics such as talking nonsense for hours, throwing out months of work on MPs' important private bills by simply shouting out 'object', and spending inordinate time debating how long we should be debating. What a waste of effort and what an insult to our voters and taxpayers. One woman aptly named this 'historic' tradition of opposition willy-jousting.

Briefly, she found Parliament taken up with pointless debate rather than the implementation of what she saw as vital reforms. "I believed I was elected to get results," she complained, "not recreate a boys' public school debating club, so I gradually withdrew from activities in the Chamber. Unfortunately the nation's women are not unaware of this time-wasting nonsense. Thanks to the televising of parliament they too can watch this unedifying spectacle. No wonder they do not rush to the ballot box."

Perhaps she dismissed her parliamentary experience too readily. After all, she *had* learned how government operates – how it is possible to effect change and initiate policy-making. This enabled her to become a consultant, specialising in advising people on how to petition the government, devise strategies and launch campaigns on behalf of causes that had been treated tardily or needed to be brought to the fore.

Having fought battles on behalf of medical charities and raised money for overseas aid, Tess had witnessed politics at the sharp end. Many of these issues were stressful and harrowing and, from time to time, for an interval of relaxation, she would take up a favourite diversion, glancing into archives of old, unsolved crimes, chief of which were the 'Walton' or Lower Quinton Murder which to this day remains unsolved, and a ritually related slaughter, the Hagley Wood (or 'Bella in the Wych Elm') case.

Looking into the misdeeds of yesteryear, Tess told me, was almost nostalgic. In contemplating a historic wrongdoing, she could sink into a sepia reverie of pure escapism. By comparison with the wars, famines and nuclear agendas agitating the event horizon of international politics, they seemed satisfyingly apart and harmless, more akin to human crossword puzzles than active, threatening presences. Time had drawn the poison from most, but that was not true of the Walton Murder – a savage, seemingly pointless homicide that remained bloody and ominous because no one had come within breathing distance of a solution. Hence Tess admitted that she experienced a quiver of horror as she burrowed deeper – a feeling of 'Should I *really* be looking into all this?' Such anxieties, however, did not prevent her going up to Warwick to examine the police records, finding the staff open and helpful:

In terms of the Walton archives I spent several days with the Warwickshire Police and went through everything. It was wheeled out on a small trolley and is really just half a dozen badly maintained files. I couldn't photocopy much but took handwritten notes of the important parts – including the interview with Potter (very sparse and not convincing one way or the other). I also have a copy of the autopsy report (brief) and pictures; went through dozens of other witness interviews from the land army girls stationed at the Potter's farm to the Prisoner of War camps nearby.

The Walton murder is a rather special murder, only the word 'special' has a polite, ceremonious echo, as if referring to a wedding anniversary and not a savage, apparently motiveless assault on an old man. What makes it stand out? Firstly, like several of Sherlock Holmes's select crimes, it takes place in the depths of the smiling countryside; secondly it has weird ritual aspects and astounding coincidences (or synchronicities) that make one think this is surely the plot of an imaginative novelist and not a slice of criminal history; thirdly it challenged the brain of the most dashing detective of the day, Inspector Robert Fabian of Scotland Yard; fourthly it brought forth the witchcraft expertise of that splendid Egyptologist and folklorist, Margaret Murray, and fifthly no one was able to pinpoint the murderer.

The Margaret Murray angle appealed to Tess. She admired the early work of that spirited archaeologist and anthropologist, especially the fieldwork on burial sites that she did with Flinders Petrie and his wife in Egypt – notably the Osirion at Abydos. Despite health problems and the responsibility of growing family, Tess decided to take a degree in archaeology at London University. She found being a student again as demanding as it was fascinating and, several years on, finished her MA and was awarded the 'UCL Margaret Murray Prize' – "that woman again, synchronicity" – for Egyptology:

I'm starting a PhD in September – a joint Forensics and Archaeology research project on disarticulated burials in prehistoric Egypt and Malta – could give me some interesting expertise to look at the Walton autopsy report again as I'll have to complete the MSc course in forensic archaeology/anthropology as part of the research… It will also entail going through the Margaret Murray archives at the Warburg Institute since she was a key archaeologist in both Malta and Egypt on the burials I will study – so I'll have my eyes open! I'm sure there must be something there about her wartime connections etc. All the occult fraternity seemed to be enmeshed.

Certain branches of archaeology – notably forensic detection – strike echoes with contemporary TV programmes like 'Silent Witness' in that the pathologist is trying to establish the cause of death, whether natural, forced or the result of an unexpected assault, by measuring, dating and chemical analysis. Tess was interested in this technique applied to mummies and skeletons:

Archaeology is fine at objectifying and depersonalising the dead and I'm interested in trying to reconstruct as much of their circumstances, manner of death and as much of their identity as possible. I'll also have a few things to say about treatment of the remains – the early Egyptian bodies were all separated out into component parts – so a box of femora here, a box of skulls there – degrading and insensitive for a people who clearly felt so strongly about integrity of the body. Many of these disarticulated burials in Egypt appear to have died violent deaths and are complete anomalies in large burial sites where the other remains are fully articulated – raises queries about sacrifice or 'laying the dead' if the death was violent or untimely.

In the middle of this dialogue with Tess, I was struck by a shattering illness that I – somehow – recovered from. Around then, I noted a book on the Constance Kent murder case by Kate Summerscale, *The Suspicions of Mr Whicher*, was topping the bestseller list. Surely the Walton Murder, with its pastoral gloom and down-at-heel wartime setting, was equally appalling?

9

Temple of Set I explored by Flinders &
Hilda Petrie & Margaret Murray.

Unfortunately it lacked the courtroom tension and the final, dramatic exposure of the culprit, leaving the Damoclean sword hanging above the village to this day. Nevertheless, it was due for a reappraisal and fresh airing, and no one knew more about it than Tess, so I contacted her to learn how things were progressing:

In relation to the book, I agree its time might have come. Even Tony Robinson (with whom I've had contact before) recently did a series on unexplained 'occult' crimes. I've been thinking about it a good deal recently and also wondering what you were up to. But I simply won't have the time to do the book. No chance I suppose that you want to do it and I could provide what info I have and feed in as necessary? I'd love to still dig around, stay connected on the periphery and help the research but I couldn't undertake the project. It's a fantastic story – I get the strong feeling (don't laugh!) that I'm never going to get off the hook on this one until someone does something!

With the recent relaxation of protocol, the National Archives presently allow access to documents formerly inaccessible. Tess thought this a good time to resume research, but she still had too much to do in the archaeological field. She was disappointed that she was not able to see the project through, but also relieved.

For at times she felt she was "tinkering on the edge" and didn't have the inclination to go further without spooking herself. She also noted how the peripheral information arising from the Lower Quinton and Hagley Wood murders throws out more intriguing leads and intricate conspiracies than the bleak facts of the crimes.

It is possible to see them as stark, brutal acts of desecration on the human body that have attracted squalls of gossip and insinuation, yet never a clear solution. This has spurred unofficial investigators to pounce upon them, develop theses and arguments in so profuse and detailed a way that it may appear they are not so much interested in solving the crime as finding a repository for the macabre scholarship rattling around in their heads.

In what follows, I have presented the facts of the case, but also deferred to the tradition of previous treatments by including the occult speculation that inevitably accompanies any re-telling.

In the past, the latter has overwhelmed the circumstantial detail. As Inspector Robert Fabian was quick to realise, when there's a dearth of evidence and a superabundance of theorising, an investigation is going badly wrong. Those drawn to the supernatural have poured a great deal of what they know into both murders and, as a result, they are now part of the Gothic-Nightmare heritage of the British Isles: half fact, half fable, standing beside films like *The Wicker Man* and the legends of Springheel Jack, Sawney Beane and Jack the Ripper. This disconcerting underworld has its roots deep in the national identity, the underbelly of empire, where shadows of violence, torture and oppression lurk, the hidden face of civic pride, where hang out the serial killer, the drug fiend and pedophile.

I do not regard myself as a student of murder or an authority on the criminal mind. When a publisher invited me to treat the subject, I explained how, through Tess's earlier hard work, I had acquired material on the Walton and Bella cases. But he had not heard of them and was not interested in single crimes for marketing reasons.

Apparently it is easy to promote encyclopaedic compilations containing multiple slayings, but a single dish of homicide is a paltry *hors d'oeuvre* to the enthusiast proper who prefers a banquet of corpses. To narrowly select is to exclude a swathe of potential readers, but it is inevitable if a fuller treatment is intended. Why these two cases interest me is that they draw in characters and personalities that elevate them into other fascinating areas: social and literary history, occultism, folklore, anthropology, spying and topography.

The title, incidentally, is taken from the chapter in Robert Fabian's book dealing with the Walton Murder.

FEBRUARY 14th, 1945

On February 14th 1945, as fire-storms ravaged Dresden and the tatters of the Germany army started to break cover and surrender, Charles Walton, aged 74, a hedger and ditcher of Lower Quinton, Warwickshire was found dead on the slopes of Meon Hill in Warwickshire after being subject to the most brutal attack, struck repeatedly by a stick, slashed and punctured by a billhook and left to die with a pitchfork pinning him through the neck.

Compared with World War 2, it was the merest ripple. Yet it "shattered the peace" of the small village. Some point out that Lower Quinton had already forfeited much of its tranquillity. Hemmed in on the west by a massive POW camp at Long Marston, the sky vibrated with the drone of aircraft and the roads were cruised by vehicles of the military. While retaining their community spirit, the villagers had been shaken out of their rural idyll and learned to busily co-ordinate their activities for the 'war effort'.

Charles Walton

Like other small and large places, Lower Quinton had endured rationing, recruitment and lighting restrictions. By 1945, when it was broadly accepted the Germans had lost, there was an atmosphere of nervous tension. People were anxious that the hostilities should cease, so that their relatives and loved ones in the army might return. But on the political front, things proceeded with a detailed deliberation that eroded the spirit. The terms of the new peace had to be worked out and approved.

Against this routine, dispirited atmosphere, Charles Walton continued to do the work he had done as boy, ditching and trimming hedges. By now, he was like a character out of *The Woodlanders* by Thomas Hardy. He belonged to and blended with the landscape that had shaped and prompted almost all his actions and decisions. Everyone in the village knew him as they might a sturdy, resilient oak. Not a great talker, his conversation was liable to arise from context and necessity rather than affability.

Presently he was sharing a half-timbered thatched cottage by the church with his niece, Edith, who was courting a man called Edgar Goode. She had lived with her uncle since she was three. They rented the property for three shillings a week. Edith or 'Edie' had a job as a printer's assembler at the RSA (Royal Society of Arts), Lower Quinton, while Charlie took on occasional jobs in fine weather for Farmer Potter who had been farming in Lower Quinton for around five years. He lived nearby at The Firs with his wife and son, Ivor.

That morning, St Valentine's Day, Edie wrapped up a chunk of cake for her uncle in a blue sugar bag. Old Charlie was wearing his usual hedging clothes: tweed jacket, grey flannel trousers with blue overall trousers over them, waistcoat, a heather cardigan and a cap. Aside from his walking stick, he would have carried his working tools, a slash-hook and trouncing fork, for trimming and uprooting, and these probably slowed his progress.

Saying goodbye to his niece, he set off from his cottage around 9 am. The weather had been freezing, but now the sun was up, warming the fields and easing the pain of agricultural toil. Bent over and crippled with rheumatism, he crept past the church, over the fields to Hillground, on the slope of Meon Hill, some three quarters of a mile from his cottage in Lower Quinton. The hedge there needed cutting back on behalf of his employer, Alfred Potter, a broad, burly man who liked to watch cricket and go to the races in his spare time. Potter's interest in horses was shared by Walton who as a young man had excelled as a horse trainer. He may have gone so far as to master the much-publicised skill of 'horse-whispering', and that in turn later gave rise to a multitude of rumours concerning the ease and skill with which he related to animals.

Around nine hours later, at 6 pm, Edie returned from work at the printers and found the cottage empty. It was not like her uncle not to be in by this time – he always finished around 4 pm. His rheumatism had been troubling him of late. He tended to walk with his shoulders bent over, arthritic hand clawing a walking stick, and she feared he might have fallen and injured himself. So she went out and alerted her neighbours, in case they had seen him.

After making a few quick enquiries that disclosed nothing, she called on a farm-worker and friend, Mr Harry Beasley, who agreed to go out with her and look around. They searched the familiar locales – Charlie was nowhere to be seen. So, around 7 pm, they went up to The Firs, the farm of his employer, Mr Alfred Potter, who appeared surprised that Walton had not yet returned. "He must have left the fields hours ago," he said. "Maybe he's had an accident, knocked down on the road or something."

The obvious place to check was the strip of hedge Charlie had been trimming when seen last. Potter found a torch and the three went out, the two men leading and Edie following. Potter quickly reached the strip of hedge on the slope of Meon Hill. A flash of torch exposed a body lying in the top right-hand corner of the field, close to an old willow "in a bit of a ditch". The two men gaped at the battered, terrified features of Old Charlie.

Potter turned, saying to Evie – "You mustn't look!"

Evie, stricken with shock, screamed loudly and Beasley tried to calm her, making sure that she did not come closer. Coincidentally a man named Harry Peachey was passing on the other side of the hedge and Beasley called to him, drawing attention to Walton's body and urging him to contact the police.

The body was lying against the hedge with Walton's bloodstained walking-stick lying nearby. The bruises on his head suggested an initial attack from that implement, knocking the old man down. Then the killer had grabbed the billhook the old man was carrying and slashed his throat with it, terminating his massacre by pinning the body to the ground with the two-tined pitchfork, also part of Walton's hedging equipment. The tines of the pitchfork pierced the flesh on either side of the victim's neck. The billhook with which the throat had been cut was stuck deep in the chest.

Not long after 7 pm, PC Lomasney arrived at Hillground, noting that Potter seemed "very upset" as well as shivering and complaining of being cold. The first medical man to examine the body was Dr A.R. McWhinney at 7.30 pm, followed at 11.30 pm by Professor J. M. Webster of the West Midlands Forensic Laboratory.

The latter was a highly experienced pathologist whose forensic analyses had solved many complex cases. After moving the body clear of the hedge to get a proper look, he identified the cause of death as shock and haemorrhage, owing to injuries dealt by a cutting and a stabbing weapon. The deep incisions told him the cutting weapon had been wielded three times. So severe was the slash across the throat the great blood vessels of the neck had been severed. Marks on the hands showed that the old man had attempted to defend himself. He estimated the time of death, 1 pm – 2pm.[1]

THE CAREER OF ROBERT FABIAN

Initially the enquiry was placed in the hands of Superintendent Simmons of Stratford-upon-Avon. But when it became apparent that finding the murderer might be a long, complicated process, the most celebrated detective of the day was assigned the case: Inspector Robert Fabian of Scotland Yard, later immortalised as 'Fabian of the Yard' in a popular TV series.

A notable incongruity was the sheer gruesome savagery of the assault. It contrasted with the victim's innocuous and peaceable nature. From the report in the Stratford-upon-Avon *Herald*, Charlie Walton emerged as a quiet-living, inoffensive old man who was well-liked by his neighbours. In spite of suffering from rheumatism and walking with the aid of sticks, he still did small jobs from time to time and was respected as a local character. Why on earth would anyone do that to him?

Inspector Robert Fabian was one of a select body of policemen who helped maintain the reputation of Scotland Yard as the headquarters of one of the finest police forces in the world. Born in 1901, he did not start out from a privileged position, attending an elementary school in Catford. Intending to follow his father, at twelve he was sent to the Borough Polytechnic to train as an engineering

---

[1] Tess Kingham commented – 'From my studies, rigor has its onset about 2 to 6 hours post-mortem and spreads over the next 4 to 6 hours to all the muscles of the body. Its most important determinants are ambient temperature and metabolic state at time of death. Cold weather delays it, while vigorous activity can speed it up slightly. I really can't see how Webster could state with confidence that the post-mortem interval was a one hour window.' The figures allow a 6–12 hour range. A mean estimate, 9 hours, would place Walton's death at 2.30 pm.

draughtsman but, although he tried hard, the work failed to inspire him. He was confined indoors most of the time and wanted to get out and do something more active and personally engaging.

One evening in 1921, he came home and found sitting in his parents' living room a very large man drinking a cup of tea. It was a family friend, Inspector Frederic Rolfe. Young Fabian listened to Fred recounting his adventures, nabbing villains and tracing them to their lairs, and decided that such exciting work might better suit his temperament. So he filled in an application at Lewisham Police Station where they measured him as 5 feet 10 inches tall and over ten stone in weight. He was also of "pure British descent", able to read, write and show a reasonable proficiency at dictation and simple arithmetic. Following a stiff medical, he was accepted, put through an intensive programme of training and then posted to the old Vine Street Police Station where he was immediately put on night duty. There he picked up the skills of observation, especially at night, paying great attention to each doorway, shadow at the window or shifting, hurrying figure who passed. Soon he learned the basics of the beat and set his mind on rising through the ranks.

After making a few arrests and proving able and efficient, he became a detective at Scotland Yard and was placed on his first murder case. Early in 1926, when he was 25 years old, he was sent to look into the criminal antics of various notorious London clubs. Being young and innocent-looking, Fabian was chosen as a 'plant'. He was told to hang about in various dens of vice and see what gossip he could pick up. A rather correct, prim young man, who did not smoke or drink, he was nicknamed by the French girls in one of the little underground clubs, 'The Little Water Drinker'. When a shooting was reported at the notorious Cochon Club, Fabian was given the assignment and promptly solved the case of 'Mad Emile and Charles the Acrobat'.

After that auspicious start, he became more and more successful and, by the time of the Walton Murder, his professional career was peaking.

Five years earlier, on 6th February 1940, he had been decorated at Buckingham Palace by King George VI with the Police Medal for Gallantry for overseeing the dismantling of a bomb in Piccadilly Circus. Supreme tribute as it was, he was probably more flabbergasted when for that same deed he received a mysterious phone call – "Have you got a minute to spare, guvnor?" – directing him to a mysterious

16

billiard saloon. He went there and stepped into a room that contained the very cream of the scum of London's villains. A huge glass of whisky and a cigar were pushed into his hands and a large gangland leader – thick fingers glittering with diamonds – held up his hand for silence and made a speech, thanking Fabian for saving the lives of some of the crooks who were at their work on the night the bomb was neutered; after that, he presented Fabian with an elegant bronze medal, the size of a penny, hanging on a blue silk ribbon with a laurel wreath on one side and inscribed on the other:

> To Detective Inspector Bob Fabian
> For Bravery, 24-6-39
> From the Boys

Fabian kept both medals in the same drawer, as if he valued them equally. But having acquired a nation-wide reputation, he did not feel especially challenged in taking on the Walton Murder. A brutal intrigue in a closed community was small beer compared with tackling the burglars, thieves, forgers and poisoners of the metropolis. The location – the small, tight community of Lower Quinton in Warwickshire where, he imagined, everyone knew each other's business and gossiped fulsomely – would make it relatively easy to solve and, indeed, the basic facts were not complex.

He was feeling rather pleased with himself at the time. Under his command, the Flying Squad had arrested a notoriously violent gang with £4,000 worth of stolen goods. It was late at night when he saw a note tucked under his telephone informing him to contact the CID Commander – apparently Warwickshire's Chief Constable had requested the help of Scotland Yard.

At 5 am he phoned the night-duty inspector at Whitehall to have someone check the torches in one of the murder bags that were packed with every device – rubber gloves for handling the corpse, handcuffs, magnifying glass and writing materials.

When he arrived in Lower Quinton with his assistant, Sergeant Webb, it was not yet dawn. The headlights from the police car were reflected in the night dew on the grass by the roadside. It was a cold, bleak February day with damp muffling the air and oil wicks glowing at the windows of cottages.

"They're waking up," remarked Superintendent Spooner of the Warwickshire police who had joined the pair at Leamington. The three of them got out and hurried to the crime scene. On reaching Hillground, what met their eyes was a not especially revealing mess of grass clogged with bloodstains mixed in with hazel and hawthorn twigs. A young constable was standing guard over the crime scene but the body itself been carried – using a five-barred gate as a stretcher – to Professor Webster's laboratory in Birmingham.

THE HENDON METHOD

An incident room was set up at nearby Stratford-upon-Avon Police Headquarters, from where Fabian directed his own enquiry, taking in daily feedback. At night, he retired to his room at a local inn and read up on the region's history. In a book titled *Warwickshire* by Clive Holland (1906), he learned that slashing a cross into the skin of a witch or warlock after they had been murdered stopped them rising from the grave. With evidence like this to digest, he realised this case might turn out unlike any other.

On the wall of the HQ at Stratford, Fabian mounted a map, transferring the details gleaned from the many photographs. Using map pins and little coloured flags and threads, he plotted the last hours of Walton's life. He put a cross on the place where the body was found – roughly an equal distance from the road at Upper Quinton on the west and Meon Lane on the east. From Charles Walton's cottage to the ditch where his body lay was around three-quarters of a mile.

Fabian was trying to establish what took place with a strong degree of certainty. That way, when he had to question suspects, he would be able to pick out anything dubious or shaky. This was the latest method taught by the Hendon school of detection: obtain the most thorough knowledge of the victim's whereabouts, personal contacts, minor details of dress and ornamentation, just before the murder. What is obvious is that, apart from the instant contamination of the crime scene by the footsteps of Edie Walton, Harry Beasley, Farmer Potter (who may have touched both the trouncing-hook and hayfork), the Warwickshire constabulary and Professor Webster – making any imprint of the murderer's footsteps almost impossible to trace – the enquiry was conducted with great thoroughness and zeal.

The police harnessed the skills of the RAF and army, using a camera-fitted Avro Anson that hovered over Meon Hill, taking shots that picked out paths, nearby farms and access points. It honed in on the field and ditch where Walton's body was found, picking over the bloodstains on the grass as khaki-clad men from the Royal Engineers walked slowly over the fields, sweeping the ground with mine detectors in hope of recovering Walton's missing watch or any other clue.

Another major check was on those living in the vicinity of the murder field. The nearest house was a cottage 300 yards away, occupied by Miss Feronia Gough, aged 33, and Mr Walter Weaver, aged 59. On the day of the murder, she had been engaged on domestic duties at the house of Mrs Nicholls at Upper Quinton, while Mr Weaver who, like Edie Walton, was employed at the printing work of the RSA at Lower Quinton, returned to the house for a mid-day meal around 1.08 pm and remained there with Miss Gough until 2 pm when they left together. Neither of them saw anyone pass their cottage or saw anything unusual in the fields nearby.

Both of their statements were verified: hence there was no connection with the fate of Charles Walton.

Similarly another couple occupied a caravan that had a clear view of the site of the murder: Flight Lieutenant Thomas Arthur Woodward and his wife Maud Dorothy Woodward. Just before he left to go on duty at Long Marston Aerodrome, he saw Charles Walton on his way to work pass his caravan at around 8.15 am. Mrs Woodward remained in the caravan all day, saying that she saw nobody in the fields at any time after Charles Walton had passed in the morning. However, she was busy attending to her baby most of the time, so that does not mean that nothing could have been going on. For instance, she did not see Alfred Potter who said that he entered the field adjacent to the one in which Walton was murdered at around 12.20 pm.

In addition, two elderly residents, Miss Charlotte Byway, aged 73, and Mr Joseph Waters, aged 83, saw Walton pass through the churchyard at 9 am and 9.30 am respectively.[2]

---

[2] The variant time-keeping is confusing but not necessarily suspicious. Flight Commander Woodward suggested an early start for Walton (8.15 am) while the elderly couple said that he arrived over an hour later (9.30 am). Fabian found nothing significant in the discrepancy, putting it down to 'honest mistakes' on the part of witnesses. Charles Walton was generally said to have set off each morning around 9 am.

Who else was around the scene of the crime on February 14th?

Henry Hall, a farm labourer of Meon Hill, watched a soldier collecting booby traps on Meon Hill at about 11 am. George Purnell, a farm labourer of Upper Quinton, saw a British Officer and a civilian walking from the direction of the hill at the same time.

These were identified as Lieutenant Alan Edwards of the 23rd I.T.C., Sergeant George Mills and Lance Corporal George Hobbis of the Royal Warwickshire Regiment. The lieutenant was in charge of manoeuvres at Meon Hill that day and Lance Corporal Hobbis was engaged in removing booby traps that had been set the previous day. They left Meon Hill just after 11 am and the district at about 2 pm.

In passing, Hobbis mentioned that about 11 am he saw a youth, Basil Hall, ploughing a field on Meon Hill and, about the same time, a man aged 60 – 70, five feet and four inches in height, dressed in a dark suit, wearing a light-coloured cap and carrying a walking stick, moving along a fence towards Meon Hill Farm, about a mile south of the scene of the crime. The youth was the son of Richard Hall, who had a farm at Meon Hill, and was ploughing in a field overlooking Upper Quinton from 10 am to 6 pm and saw nobody save a man at about 3 pm. He was standing by a hedge about 150 yards from where he was ploughing and appeared to be looking towards Lower Quinton church, staying there for about half an hour.

The older man seen by Lance Corporal Hobbis was John Henry Field, aged 64, a farm labourer employed by Mr Frank Stanley who also had a farm at Meon Hill. Mr Field visited Meon Hill almost every morning to attend the cattle; that day he was dressed in the manner previously described and carrying a walking stick.

The only other person working in the vicinity of the murder was George Higgins, aged 72, of Fair View, Lower Quinton, who worked for Mr Valender of Upper Quinton as an odd job man. A lifetime friend of Charles Walton, for a number of years they had worked together at hedge-cutting, yet they had not seen each other since the previous Christmas. On the day of the murder, George Higgins had started work at Valender's farm at 8.30 am, engaged mainly in the barn until mid-day, when he had his lunch in the bakehouse. In the afternoon he returned to the barn to work until 4 pm.

Fabian noted that Higgins in the course of his work would have recourse to Mr Valender's field that was only 300 yards from where Charles Walton was working: "So far as opportunity is concerned, George Higgins could have quite easily committed the murder and returned to his work without his absence having been noticed."

But Higgins was a frail old man, small in stature, partially crippled and there was "no evidence other than he was always on the friendliest terms with the deceased", so he would hardly qualify as a suspect.

One final point, those who saw Walton that morning made no mention of his working tools, his slash-hook or trouncing fork. Such tools, it has been pointed out, were usually left by field workers in position, hidden under a hedge or covered nearby. But this was Walton's *first* morning of the work in question; to have earlier placed them in position would have necessitated two journeys unless he had been informed in advance. Farmer Potter had last paid him £2.15s for the fortnight ending February 10th. So it is probably correct to assume that Walton was carrying his tools on the morning of February 14th, 1945.

POTTER QUESTIONED

S uspicion fell on Alfred Potter from the beginning. PC Lomasney observed the farmer's agitation when he appeared on the crime scene, but thought that he was overplaying things – "I think Potter appeared more worried than one would have expected him to be."

Alfred Potter

He reasoned that Potter was used to blood – slaughtering and castrating was part of his profession. For him to be so bothered by cold weather was odd considering his occupation took him out to attend animals at all hours and in all kinds of weather. Bearing in mind the tragic circumstances, a greater commitment and curiosity might have been expected, especially as the murdered man was his employee who had been carrying out his orders.

The first interview with Farmer Alfred Potter took place at 11 pm on the day of the murder and was conducted by Detective Inspector Toombs of the Warwickshire Constabulary. Potter, aged forty, managed a farm called The Firs on behalf of his father: L.L. Potter & Sons was the official name of the business. The land he worked was owned by Magdalen College, Oxford, to whom rent was paid. He had been employing Walton casually for around nine months; the old man worked only in fine weather.

On the day of the murder, he visited the College Arms, leaving at 12 noon and crossing to a field adjoining Hill Ground from where Walton could be seen working, attending to a hedge about 500 or 600 yards away. He only had about ten yards more hedge to cut. Later he attended to a dead heifer that required removal.

This statement was elaborated three days later, in an interview with Detective Sergeant Webb. Then he said that, after leaving the College Arms, he went across to a field on his farm called Cack Leys to check the sheep and feed some calves. When he reached the field, it was about 12.10 pm and he noticed Walton working in his shirtsleeves in the next field, about 500 yards away. This was the only time that he had seen Walton so lightly attired and he remarked to himself, "He's getting on with it today!" Potter added: "I would have gone over to have seen him, but I had a heifer in a ditch nearby which I had to attend to. I went straight back home and got there at about twenty-to-one. I then went to see the heifer."

Later that day, at 6.15 pm, Miss Walton and Mr Beasley called on him and explained that Charles had not returned home. Potter then went out with them to look for him and found his body about ten yards from where he had seen the old man working at 12.20 pm.

Potter's statement was read back to him and he commented: "Although I cannot be positive I am almost certain it was Walton who I saw working at the hedge at twenty past twelve on the 14th February, 1945."

Attempts by the police to verify Potter's statement revealed the heifer he mentioned was found dead on 13th February, 1945, and not removed from Firs Farm until the late afternoon of 14th February, 1945. This was confirmed by the other farmworkers who referred to the arrangements for the collection and removal of the carcase.

By then, Fabian had collected Walton's clothing from the West Midland Forensic Science Laboratory and found that the shirtsleeves had been cut away above the elbows and that the woollen cardigan he wore over it had long sleeves. "It therefore," he concluded, "would have been impossible for Potter to have seen him working in his shirtsleeves on the day of the murder. I had also borne in mind that, although Potter had spoken of Charles Walton working in his shirtsleeves at 12.20 pm, when the latter was murdered, shortly afterwards he was dressed in his jacket, as can be proved by the cut in the shoulder caused by the trouncing-hook and the blood with which the clothing was saturated. It seems very improbable that, if Charles Walton was working in his shirtsleeves at 12.20 pm, he would suddenly decide to put his jacket on unless he had made up his mind to finish work for the day."

Fabian's suspicions were aroused. As a witness, Potter was halting and far from precise, replying to leading questions in a blurred, unsatisfactory way, while volunteering useless, extraneous detail. As an employer, he was not exemplary either. Two of his previous workers, William George Dyde and George Purnell, complained that he was not a reliable payer and that he had evaded their requests. Potter admitted to Fabian there had been were times when Walton had asked for his wages and he, through overspending, was not able to oblige, the last such occasion being Christmas 1944. He always did settle up, "later in the week" he emphasised.

To improve his local knowledge, Fabian spoke to PC Lomasney whose beat covered Upper and Lower Quinton, and who for some time had been on friendly terms with Potter. The latter reported a conversation with Potter on 20th February, concerning fingerprints on the murder weapons. Potter became anxious, emphatic. "I have told the police," he said, "that I caught one of the tools with my hand to see what had happened. I told them more than once. They know that."

This admission brought forth disapproval from Lilian, Potter's wife, who thought such a thing was best left unsaid.

PC Lomasney was sure that this was the *first* time Potter had mentioned handling the murder weapons. It was as if he was trying to pre-empt any possibility of suspicion attaching itself to him. He became very excited when a serviceman came to the door, telling him that an Italian POW from the camp had been detained on suspicion: "Potter affected great glee and his wife became almost hysterical with delight."

Three days later, yet another statement was taken from Potter at Stratford-upon-Avon Police Station. He admitted to making one or two 'mistakes' in his earlier statement of the 17th February.

After he had been to Cack Leys, apparently to see the sheep and feed the calves, he had gone home, sat down and read the paper for about five minutes, then went out into the cowshed to help Batchelor, the cowman, finish pulping some mangolds, feeding the machine for about five minutes until Batchelor asked him the time.

When detectives took possession of Potter's clothing, which included his Bedford cord breeches, the farmer remarked: "You may find some blood on the knees. I got it there when I took a calf from a cow last Monday." But the garment had been very thoroughly washed. This was underlined by Professor Webster, the chief forensic scientist, who examined it and found "two areas upon the breeches which gave presumptive tests for blood but they had been so well cleaned that it was impossible to say whether or not this blood had been human or not."

No physical evidence was visible on Potter. No one noted scratches or abrasions on his arms – for the old man *had* put up a struggle. What irked Fabian were the irritating variations in his statements. The farmer was too keen to provide non-significant details about Walton's shirtsleeves or the dead heifer.

EVIDENCE OF LILIAN POTTER

Potter's wife, Lilian Elizabeth Potter, aged 40, spoke of her husband's movements on the 14th February, saying he entered the house about 11 am to fetch implements to castrate some calves, staying only a few minutes and returning after 12.30 pm and reading the paper for some minutes. He asked, "How long will dinner be?" She told him it would not be long and he said, "I've got to go and help 'Happy' [Batchelor] to pulp some mangolds" and left the house about 12.40 am. Lilian Potter was sure of this because of the wireless and the clock. Potter came back for his dinner at 1.05 pm. The baker's roundsman called while they were having a cup of tea after dinner and joined them. At 2.10 pm or 2.15 pm, Potter left and returned shortly to telephone about the removal of the heifer.

Fabian commented:

It is remarkable that, while Mrs Potter is so certain of the exact time her husband came and went round about dinner time, she cannot recall what they had for dinner or to be sure of any other times during that day. It will be noted that although she states that she was in the house all day and mentions that her husband came to the house to fetch some castrating implements at 11 am, she says nothing about him returning some tools shortly after 12 noon as stated by her husband at the inquest.

On the day after the murder, Mrs Potter confirmed that her husband admitted touching the billhook to PC Lomasney after Mr Beasley had

25

asked him to establish that Mr Walton was dead. Referring to her husband's breeches, she said that she was sure her husband had never cleaned them, prompting Fabian to conclude that Potter had trained his wife to produce information that pretty well corroborated what he had told the police.

However, despite an element of artful management, Fabian could not dismiss the foregoing as a tightly contrived lie, Potter's testimony being confirmed by Joseph Stanley, a farmer of Lower Quinton, who had arranged to help Potter on the 14th February with the castration of two calves. Afterwards the two of them went for a drink at the College Arms. Potter had a couple of Guinnesses while they were there from 11.45 am to 12 noon. The two were later seen by Mr John Henry Field, a farm labourer earlier referred to, who passed Mr Stanley's garage at about 12 noon and observed Potter and Stanley looking over a tractor.

After that, there was a crucial gap that vexed Fabian:

Every effort has been made to check Potter's movement that morning but, other than his wife, who says he returned to the house at 'some time after half-past twelve', nobody can say they saw him from about 12 noon until 12.40 pm when Batchelor fixes the time by the fact that he and Potter went to look at the church clock and it was then 1 pm. Potter, himself, says that he helped Batchelor for about five minute before looking at the church clock and it therefore appears far more likely that it was later than 12.40 am when Batchelor first saw Potter.

However, the fact remains that, whatever Potter did between 12 noon and 1 pm, he would have had ample time to have committed the murder for, by his own admission, he was in the adjoining field by 12.10 pm, and after returning home sat down and looked at the paper for about five minutes.

Potter, as might be expected, made plain to the police and coroner that he liked and got on with Walton:

"All the time I have known Charles Walton, I have never had a cross word with him and I have never known him to be in a temper. I have never heard him say a bad thing about anybody and I don't think he had an enemy in the world. He was a man of spirit and, if attacked, I think he would have retaliated. He was respected by everybody and I have never known him to enter a public house."

"When he wasn't at work, he was at home. I have never seen him in the company of anyone. His only friend, so far as I know, was George Higgins who lives at Lower Quinton. They used to go for walks sometimes on a Sunday."

This is flat to the point of blandness. It is as if quiet, self-contained, self-effacing characters like Walton merge into the background and people are only able to recall their unobtrusiveness. There were hints that Walton had a short temper when the occasion demanded and there is a glint of that in Potter's concession he was "a man of spirit" but he offers no anecdote or memory to illustrate this. What is clear is that Walton as a personality *was* something of a 'mystery', and what was 'empty' or unknown about him was to be rapidly be filled in with a mix of authentic recollection, gossip, speculation and fiction.

PRISONERS OF WAR

Absence of motive was the detectives' problem. Who'd kill a gnarled old man going about his daily toil in the late evening of his life? It was an outrage that seemed to run counter to the decorum of natural law. Within a few years, the shadows would have claimed him as their own and the earth taken him in gently. So why this violent intrusion, this flagrant disruption of the natural course, so that a person who had lived so humbly and inconspicuously, in apparent harmony with birds and nature, should meet a blood-spattered fate that more befitted a doomed tyrannical king in a Greek tragedy?

At the beginning Fabian thought the investigation would not be especially complex. It was a small village, less than 500 people; everyone knew everyone else's business. They would quickly crack under professional questioning and he would return to London. But the investigation did not proceed with the coherent swiftness he had anticipated. The circumstantial evidence was paltry, the forensic traces meagre and, what with the large number of POWs in the vicinity, establishing everyone's whereabouts was wearily demanding. Reverting to the tried-and-tested approach of re-examining the crime scene in hope of locating an overlooked clue, Fabian took the route Charles Walton followed to his death over and over again. Simply he was going round in circles rather than penetrating to the centre.

Joseph Stanley, an old farmer who had once employed Walton, was convinced the detectives were deluded. As he saw it, the community of Lower Quinton was wholly innocent: "This is a small community. We all know what's going on. Is it someone in the village? I don't think so. Someone would have got to know something if the man they are looking for is still here. I tell you they're looking in the wrong place."

Suspicion naturally fell on the large number of foreign prisoners quartered in the huge camp at Long Marston and elsewhere in the region. By the end of the war, England was containing some 40,000 POWs, none of whom managed to escape, but there were various uprisings and fights at the many camps over the country.

A week previous to Charles Walton's murder, seven Germans in the north-west of England broke out – an initiative resulting in a man's death and the injuring of four others. A month later, prisoners from Atherstone in Warwickshire escaped and had to be recaptured. The obligation of having to guard so many was demanding and wearisome. Security was often slack at the camps, with inmates regularly sneaking through the gates and 'taking time off' to explore the area. There were rumours of POWs molesting women and stealing farm produce – but this was often exaggerated. The majority were not professional soldiers or seasoned lawbreakers but citizens who had been forced to enlist and fight for their countries. But as they were strangers and more than doubled the population of Lower Quinton, it was naturally whispered there was a far greater likelihood of 'one of them' killing Walton than his friends and neighbours in the village.

Farmer Potter himself was quick to hint that this would be an obvious route of enquiry for the Inspector. In Fabian's special report [30/4/45] Potter is quoted as visiting the scene of the murder on the morning after, 15th February.

Police Constable John West, of Warwickshire Country Constabulary, stated that at 5 am he relieved another officer who was guarding the murder scene. At about 7.40 am, when it had been daylight for about twenty minutes, a man came walking along the hedge that Walton had been cutting and greeted him. "Good morning, it's been a bit of a frost, ain't it?" He went on to introduce himself as Farmer Potter who had originally located the body. "It was a mess and I didn't touch him," he explained, "but I did put my fingers on the stale of the pitchfork." He added that he had sent someone to inform the police, and that he'd caught a glimpse of Walton earlier. "He was alright earlier when I came up to the cattle. I saw him from the other field."

Then he turned to the subject of the POWs and remarked: "These blasted Italians are poaching all over the place and it might be one of them. By the way, his stick and file they were looking for are up the hedge there. I saw them when I came along just now."

PC West was later interviewed by Fabian who established that he had confused the details: Potter had not admitted touching the pitchfork but the trouncing-hook.

As for the Italian POWs, they were quartered at the camp at Long Marston, two miles from Upper and Lower Quinton. There were 1045 of them, all classed as 'collaborators' and fairly unpopular with the locals who tended to pin thefts and various misdemeanours on them. A further 39 were kept at a hostel at Shipton-on-Stour and an RAF station at Long Marston housed an additional 20.

Mr George Edward Hopkins, aged 75, a general labourer working in a field about 300 yards from the POW Camp at Long Marston, reported seeing an Italian walking fast across a field towards the Camp. He said "Afternoon" as he passed, going into the back of the Camp rather than the regular entrance. The route he took was not the footpath proper, and he was picked out about two miles from the scene of the murder.

This was quickly investigated. Footprints were found along the route and plaster casts of them taken, but it was soon found that the impressions were similar to many of the boots worn by Italians that were repaired to a standard pattern.

Two other Italians were seen at Upper Quinton at 12.10 pm on the 14th February by Margaret Peachey, aged 11, who watched them cross the green and go into an alley leading to the fields. She also saw two Italians, whom she thought were the same two, in Upper Quinton at 4.20 pm. Mrs Annie Norton of Upper Quinton also saw the pair between 12 noon and I pm that day, walking towards the green. These may well have been the same Italians observed by Margaret earlier. Mrs Norton said she would not be able to identify them but, when an identification parade was set up, Margaret Peachey was able to pick out one, Roderigo Brunelli, aged 27. The latter explained that 14th February was his rest day, and he had left the camp at 2 pm, walking to Lower Quinton and then on to Upper Quinton where he met another Italian POW, Mario Chicolli, and together they went for a walk, purchasing cigarettes at the Post Office at Lower Quinton. Their testimony was later verified by Mrs Phyllis M. Collett who worked in the Post Office.

Two Italians were also seen that day at a point in Meon Lane at about 1.30 pm. A baker's roundsman, Mr John Lawrence Messer, saw two of them on the grass verge by the side of the road. One appeared to be wiping his hands whilst the other appeared to have just risen from the ground or to have come through the hedge. Though it was only a glancing encounter, Messer supplied a detailed description "even down to his teeth." One of them apparently had a look "as if he did not want to be seen" but Fabian was not convinced, dismissing Messer as "a most unsatisfactory type of witness" upon whom he placed little reliance.

But Messer might not have seemed *that* imprecise when the detectives cornered the very POW he had described – a swarthy Italian found in the camp washing blood from his coat. Swiftly he was divested of his garment that was sent to the laboratory in Birmingham, so that the blood samples might be matched with those of the murder victim. Later, a group of Royal Engineers swept their mine detectors through the hedge where he had been earlier; the groan of their motors surged into a shriek, making Fabian think: "At last, we've found Walton's old tin watch!" But instead they came across a rabbit snare laid by the same Italian whose coat, the laboratory tests revealed, was stained with rabbit's blood.

Yet another Italian POW, Calogero Bonano, surreptitiously went into Lower Quinton on a bicycle two or three times during the afternoon in order to make purchases. There may well have been others who took time off, but nearly all the occupants of the camp were interrogated by way of a translator or otherwise to the police's satisfaction.

During enquiries carried out by Superintendent Spooner, three fox snares were found by Sergeant Hinksman of the Warwickshire Constabulary, in the hedges within a few yards of the crime, but these were quickly accounted for, being laid by three seventeen-year-old local boys: Francis Smith, Geoffrey Sheppard and Thomas Russell.

Another character on whom suspicion briefly fell was Private Thomas Davies of the Long Marston Garrisons, who performed the duty of camp rat-catcher. He was suspected of being in Lower Quinton at the time of the murder and was known to have frequented the fields around Meon Hill. Although regarded "an unscrupulous type", he was cleared of any complicity in the murder by his fellow soldiers who vouched for his movements. A tramp with a ginger beard, Frederick Sandford, aged 55, who did casual work for farmers, was also interviewed on his whereabouts and a statement taken.

The enquiry was truly massive. In the Long Marston Garrison, in addition to the Italian prisoners, there were 3,093 British soldiers who had to be accounted for. Mental defectives in the area were also located and checked.

All this necessitated working both with provincial police forces and the military, but still Fabian found nothing incriminating:

From enquiries I made in this matter I have been unable to establish that any of these Italians have ever resorted to violence during their stay at Long Marston and cannot find an authentic case of them even being discourteous to the local villagers. The result of these intensive enquiries into the movements of Italians on the 14th February, 1945, does not reveal any evidence which could connect them with the murder.

Even though much of the work and translation problems were eased by the presence of Detective Sergeant Saunders, a fluent Italian speaker, it must have been one of the most exacting enquiries in the history of detection. Apart from the blundering initial examinations, when evidence from the crime scene was trampled over, no one could have accused Fabian and his team of overlooking a detail or missing a clue, but none led to the murderer. "We persevered," he recalled, "took 4000 statements, traced tinkers and gypsies. We sent 29 samples of clothing, hair, etc., of various suspects to Birmingham laboratories for analysis. I had tramps retained in Somerset, boot-repairers questioned in Salisbury, but the murder remained unsolved."

BLACK MARKET

Despite his application, Fabian never looked into the proposition that the exactions of a wartime economy – specifically the black market in meats, eggs, fruits and vegetables – was a motive for the murder. The theory was that Walton was involved in illegal trading or privy to information relating to it. The murder was intended to stop him divulging the names of the guilty parties.

This idea, first advanced by Mr W.G. Gray, has supportive details, such as the fact that Walton shared his row of houses with an abattoir that was also used by Potter. Hence facilities were on hand, but countering this Lower Quinton was surrounded by the military and was a vulnerable place from which to conduct an illegal operation. There were plenty looking out for spies and signs of underhand activity, and yet it has to be acknowledged that vehicles passing through during the cover of darkness would not have raised an eyebrow in a village that was constantly subject to movements of troops and supplies.

THE CORONER'S COURT

Charles Walton's Cottage, Lower Quinton

The scarcity of suspects was a major problem for the detectives. Alfred Potter lay at the heart of the intrigue, but apart from him the shadow of suspicion only lightly touched a soldier from an adjoining camp already mentioned and a young belligerent fellow of a powerfully depressive disposition from Lower Quinton called Smith. The latter's violent temper resulted in the battering of a man and woman in a garage. Not long after the Walton Murder, Smith left the locality and gassed himself alone. But there was no evidence, save sharing the same village, connecting him with the murder. Hence, by the time of the Coroner's Inquest [20/2/45], at Stratford-upon-Avon town hall, the only major witness was Alfred Potter who explained Walton "started when he liked and knocked off when he liked."

The farmer was not aware of Walton carrying money and remarked that he had never known him with more than a pound on his person. On the morning of the murder, he had not seen Walton going to work, only someone he thought was Walton around 12.30 pm. The Coroner (Mr George Frederick Lodder) told Potter that he would be questioned in detail as he was the last person to have seen the victim.

So Potter obliged, telling him about his visit to the public house and later seeing Walton in his shirtsleeves – a point which was challenged:

CORONER: Have you been told that Walton had no shirtsleeves?
POTTER: I am not sure it was him but I saw someone in shirtsleeves.
CORONER: Was this man using tools?
POTTER: Well, I can't say. I never saw him move. I just thought it was him at the time and moved on.
CORONER: When the body was found, did you touch it?
POTTER: No, but I got hold of his trouncing-hook.
CORONER: You cannot help further, can you?
POTTER: I am afraid not, sir. I wish I could.
CORONER: Did you get on well with Walton?
POTTER: I have never had a row with any man in this country. I just let him get on with his job and he told me what I owed him. I always trusted him.

When Fabian interrupted, pointing out Potter's evidence did not tally with an earlier account of his that had him feeding the cattle and then attending to a dead heifer, Potter admitted he'd initially got his facts wrong and his present testimony was what he'd prefer to stand by.

CORONER: One has to give you credit for being disturbed.
POTTER: I don't know what I felt. I was so cut up.
CORONER: Can you think or know of anybody the deceased was unfriendly with, or there was any quarrel with?
POTTER: None whatsoever.
CORONER: Did you see anyone else about the fields that day?
POTTER: The only people I saw were soldiers and possibly an airman or two.
CORONER: Is there anything in your fields to attract them?
POTTER: Just above there are quite a few rabbits, but not on my land.

Professor Webster declared Charles Walton had died from shock and serious cuts to the neck and throat. The old man had put up a struggle, tried to resist his attacker as was demonstrated by the wounds and scratches on the backs of his hands. The attitude of the body suggested Walton had been knocked down, then pinned to the earth with his own hay fork and dealt savage blows with the slash-hook.

The jury returned a verdict of 'murder by some person or persons unknown'.

CONFLICTING STATEMENTS

As previously alluded to, small contradictions and variations in Alfred Potter's statements had roused the suspicion of Fabian.

Firstly there was Potter's statement to Inspector Toombs on 14th February, the night of the murder. He said that he left the College Arms pub at 12 noon – he especially noted the time – and went to the small field adjoining Hill Ground (where Walton was murdered) and saw him hedging from about 500 to 600 yards away.

Secondly there was the statement made on 17th February at Stratford-upon-Avon Police Station, saying that he left the College Arms at about 12.10 pm and went across to Cack Leys where he was able to see Walton at the hedge. Later he emended this: "Although I cannot be positive I am almost certain it was Walton whom I saw working at the hedge... Whoever it was appeared to be trimming the hedge."

(Fabian commented: "It will be remembered that Potter, in his earlier statements, said that from the point where he saw Walton working to the point where he later found the body would constitute about half-an-hour's work. If the man who Potter saw was not Walton it would be interesting to know who did the half-an-hour's work on the hedge.")

Potter added that he would have gone over and spoken to Walton, but because he had to attend to a heifer in a ditch, he went straight back home, arriving there at 12.40 pm and then going to see the heifer.

By the time he made his third statement on 23rd February, the pattern had undergone a further alteration: "I went home and looked at the paper for about five minutes. I then...helped Batchelor...for about five minutes...I looked at the church clock. It was just one o clock."

All these discrepancies, Fabian pointed out, are important because they affect the time when Charles Walton was being murdered. Potter firstly stated it was pressure of work that stopped him seeing Walton at 12.20 pm, but later testified that he went home and, far from urgently attending to the heifer, read a paper and pulped mangolds with Batchelor, not getting around to arranging for the removal of the carcase until 3 pm. "Potter," Fabian emphasised, "is undoubtedly lying about his actions at this critical time but the reason for these lies can, for the present, only be a matter of conjecture."

The other great doubt raised was the matter of the trouncing-hook. In his statement on the 23rd February, Potter said: "On the 14th or the 15th of February, I had touched the trouncing-hook when I found the body. This went against the memory of PC Lomasney who said that Potter had made no mention of the tool to the police until he alluded to his fingerprints on 20th February. Explaining how he came to handle the trouncing-hook, Potter said that Beasley had said to him, "You had better have a look to see he [Charles Walton] is gone," and he had then caught hold of it. When questioned, however, Beasley denied making the remark, adding that Potter never touched the body, the trouncing-hook or hay fork. He affirmed that he had no doubt from the first glance that Charles Walton was dead and was fairly sure that Potter realised that.

As for Potter's anxiety regarding the presence of his fingerprints on the murder weapon, that turned out to be groundless: no such impressions were found. Again the police thought Potter's behaviour suspicious: was he worried that he may not have wiped the handle clean after executing the assault?

Apparently Batchelor corroborated Potter's account of 23rd February, but Fabian found it curious that he did not mention them pulping mangolds together in his earlier statement. Fabian thought Potter may have deliberately bided his time, not alluding to this until after he had seen Batchelor and established that he would vouch for him.

FOR LOVE OR MONEY

Passion and cash are thought of as major motives for murder and crime in general. Charles Walton was a long-time widower without a regular lady friend. He was crippled by rheumatism and went about his life quietly and unobtrusively. To all appearances, he was the last person likely to call forth such a blind, savage act, but the detectives made a thorough check of his income and savings and those of Alfred Potter, too, just to see if there was indication of a money motive.

The accounts of L. L. Potter & Sons were managed by Norman George Hitchman. They revealed payments to Walton over the last thirty-five weeks – on eight weeks alone he had received less than the £3 Potter claimed as his payment. Walton was infirm, never working a continuous week, only in snatches in fine weather, so the sums drawn out on his behalf by Potter were suspect. In other words, Potter was claiming too much on behalf of Walton. Fabian knew he was salting away the surplus. "Potter, by his own admission," he observed, "is guilty of claiming more wages than were due and there is no doubt that he was making a good thing out of Walton's employment by him."

And yet, if Potter practised a little imaginative accounting, that hardly points to him being a murderer. And what would have been his motive? Initially the attack on Walton was thought to be a crude and violent robbery. This was supported by the disarray of his clothing, the absence of any money on his person and the watch he habitually carried being missing.

Many locals believed Charlie Walton owned a stash of money that he had squirreled away, but upon his death his assets were only about £5. When his wife died in 1927, Walton was left £297 and early in 1928 placed £200 in a deposit account with the Stratford-upon-Avon branch of the Midland Bank. In 1936 he received £44 from a benevolent fund to which he had belonged, but although he was in good employment during this period, his money had dwindled to £2.11s.9d by 1938.

Mr Frederick C.R. Frost of Magdalen Farm, Lower Quinton, employed him for seven years prior to the Autumn of 1944, never paying him less than £3 a week, so his lack of funding at death was something of a mystery. Neither is there any report of him speaking in detail about his financial arrangements to anyone, leaving the possibility that he had hidden cash. His abrupt death prevented him from bequeathing or divulging its whereabouts.[3]

"Charles Walton," Fabian stated, "was a man of most frugal habits. His rent was but three shillings a week and his total outgoings at the most cannot be estimated at more than £2 a week. Walton did not smoke and seldom visited a public house. He was a man of solitary habits and his only known acquaintance was George Higgins whom we have already mentioned."

More pertinently, a farm-worker called Robert Hemmings insisted Old Charlie wore a money belt and always had money in the pouches. He recalled when another labourer lost a pound note the old man commented: "You shouldn't carry a lot about with you. I never do. I'm not short of three hundred pounds." This was confirmed to Fabian by another man present, Horace Yates of Willicote Cottages.

Mrs Beasley, a friend, recalled, "I lived next door to him for twenty years. I did Charles's bit of shopping for him, and I am convinced he had no more than a few shillings in his belt. But, despite his paucity of cash proper, she maintained that money was the motive behind the murder: "The murderer must have known the old man's movements and just where he would be on the afternoon when he was killed."

Edie described her uncle on February 14th, before he set off, as wearing a body belt, in which money and useful small items might be kept, and an ordinary belt, but makes no mention of it containing

---

[3] It was whispered that shopkeepers in Lower Quinton had noticed Charlie cashing cheques for sums larger than he would appear to need. In the months preceding the murder, this was said to happen repeatedly and, after his death, promoted the rumour that he was paying someone: hence the idea that he had been loaning money to Potter who killed him when he started switching up the pressure for repayment. However, no IOUs were found in his room and Charlie appears to have been a cautious, canny type rather than one to spread his money. He never confided details of any debt to Edie or his close friend, George Higgins. Nor did his alleged bout of withdrawing funds catch the eye of Fabian or any policeman who looked through his accounts.

money and Potter said that he had never known Walton go around with more than £1 on his person.

According to the crime writer Richard Whittington-Egan, who interviewed Fabian after he had retired, Edie confided that Charlie had loaned Potter money and, around the time of the murder, repayment was well overdue. This disclosure, if true, came rather late in the day.

If Edie had earlier alluded to a money feud between Charles and Alfred, making plain her willingness to testify on oath before a court of law, then the outcome of the case might have been dramatically different. So one has to treat this late-flowering 'conversation with Fabian' with caution. Clear evidence of a financial dispute would have dispelled the melodramatic speculation that lay in wait, rendering it an extraordinary murder with an ordinary motive.

WALTON MURDER – CHRONOLOGY

(9 am) Charles Walton sets off to cut the hedges at Hillground, a field on the slopes of Meon Hill.

(11 am) Potter, who has been working on his farm, goes home to collect castrating tools.

(11.45 am) Potter and Joseph Stanley go drinking in the College Arms.

(12 am) Potter leaves the College Arms.

(12 am – 12.40 pm) Fabian's 'murder interval' when no alibi observed Potter's comings and goings, of which he himself was vague, while his wife, Lilian, parroted what he had told the police, specific times being 'alleged' rather than corroborated.

(12.10 pm) Potter recalls going to Cack Leys and seeing Walton working.

(12.30 pm) According to Lilian Potter, Potter returns home, leaving ten minutes later to help Happy Batchelor pulp mangolds.

(1 pm) Potter and 'Happy Batchelor' check the church clock and Potter returns home for dinner.

(3.30 pm) Potter attends to the removal of a dead heifer.

(4 pm) Walton fails to return home. Edie becomes anxious.

(6.30 pm) Walton missing; Edie, Beasley and Potter search; find his body.

(7.15 pm) Police Constable Lomasney inspects the body of Charles Walton.

(7.30 pm) Doctor McWhinney looks over the body.

(11.30 pm) The body is examined by Professor Webster who detected some heat in the hand. Rigor mortis had not completely set in; some extremities were still flaccid. He estimated time of death as 1 pm – 2 pm.

'STANGING'

Reading Professor Webster's autopsy requires a strong stomach, but it is a primary source for anyone seriously interested in resolving this gruesome homicide:

The body was found lying on the left side with the knees bent and arms bent out to elbows; lots of blood on head. Hayfork (both prongs) and trouncing-hook buried deep into the tissues of his neck and upper thoracic cavity. His headgear had fallen off and was just below his head [so he must have been hit with stick while on ground or his hat would have fallen off before and not be under his head, so why didn't murderer just finish him off with a stick?] His left hedging glove was between his left bent elbow and his side. The right hedging glove was on the ground to the left of the body on level with the grass. There was a belt over both his legs and a broken piece of his braces on the ground just behind him. The front of his clothes was undone and the top part of his fly was open.

Near to him I noticed a bloodstained walking stick. I removed the hook and fork and it required considerable effort to pull both of these out. The hook was superimposed upon the fork and the prongs of the fork were plunged into the body a full three-quarters of their length.

The handle of the fork moreover was forced under a cross-piece in the hedge and the body had to be pulled down slightly to release this. I found that rigor mortis had not completely involved the whole body. Some of the small parts of the extremities being still flaccid. There was also even to the hand a little body warmth left. Temperature at rectum, 88° Fahrenheit.

There was considerable blood on face and ground; also other injuries to the head. It was dark so I couldn't fully examine, but later looked over the body at Stratford Mortuary. Height approx. 5ft 6ins; well-nourished but of a 'spare' type.

Large bruises (x 4) on the back of the right hand and right forearm [defence wound?]. Ante-mortem and blood had not clotted. Small abrasion on the point of the right elbow.

Flat laceration on the back of left index finger – could have been caused by the old man defending himself against a cutting implement.

No injuries to the palm of the hands. At the top of the left hand shoulder there were superficial abrasions and bruises such as could have been caused by the hayfork I saw. There were 7 lacerated wounds on the scalp, situated on the back and top of the head. None of these wounds led down to the bone. The wounds were superimposed upon deep-seated bruises on the scalp. On examination, I ascertained that the left clavicle had been completely severed at the sternum. There were 7 ribs broken on the left side.

The main wound on the neck extended from about one inch below the point of the chin down to the suprasternal notch. It was obvious this hole which measured 4¼ by 3½ inches had been made by more than one slash. The tissues on the front of the neck were grossly cut about and there was free communication between this hole and the left pleural cavity. To the left and right of the hole in the neck were the puncture wounds made by the prongs of the hayfork. I later investigated the trachea and upper air passages. This division of the respiratory tract clearly showed that three distinct blows by a cutting instrument had been delivered.

The cause of death is quite clear. He died from shock haemorrhage due to grave injuries to the neck and chest. Injuries had been caused by two types of weapon – a cutting weapon and a stabbing weapon. The cutting weapon had been wielded at least three times with great violence. The old man defended himself as is shown by the cuts on the hands and arms.

"The work of a maniac," Sergeant Webb remarked, thinking the use of the hayfork especially deranged. Yes, the policemen agreed, anyone who committed so extreme an act, for no obvious reason, was in all likelihood mentally afflicted.

However, the more reflective, experienced Superintendent Spooner drew Webb's and Fabian's attention to a disquieting rural practice, showing them a passage in a book, *Folk Lore, Old Customs and Superstitions in Shakespeare-land* (1929) by J. Harvey Bloom:

In 1875 a weak-minded young man killed an old woman named Ann Tennant with a hay-fork because he believed she had bewitched him.

A companion volume that Fabian was studying, *Warwickshire* by Clive Holland, commented:

A man name James Hayward, who stabbed to death with a pitchfork an old woman, exclaiming that he would kill all sixteen witches in Long Compton…his mode of killing was evidently a survival of the ancient Anglo-Saxon custom of dealing with witches by means of 'stacung' or sticking spikes into them.

On hearing this, Sergeant Webb laid a mock-sympathetic hand on Spooner's shoulder, saying: "The mad, hectic life of the country is proving too much for you, sir!"

Fabian slips this folkloristic flourish into his book as if it is little more than whimsical garnish, but he was demonstrating that – excellent policeman though he was – he would not have made the grade as a literary sleuth. For he was splitting in two a single item of evidence, not recognising both extracts, the Bloom and Holland, referred to the same murder, the first highlighting the victim and the second the perpetrator.

For clarification, the detailed report in *The Stratford Herald* is more helpful, explaining how, on the 15th September, 1875, a feeble-minded man named James Hayward attacked a 79-year-old woman, Ann Tennant, at Long Compton, with a pitchfork and inflicted injuries upon her of which she died three hours later. At the inquest James was said to be drunk and "suffering from delusions that people were bewitching him". He was brought to trial at Warwick Assizes, found Not Guilty upon grounds of insanity and ordered to be detained during Her Majesty's pleasure.

The assault was not identical with what Old Charlie suffered. Ann Tennant had left the local bakers and was on her way home when Hayward, who had known her family for years, stabbed her in the legs with the prongs of a pitchfork, and knocked her down with the handle. Doctor Hutchinson was called. He found the body in a dreadful state, puncture wounds on her left temple, behind the ears and on both legs. He dressed them but she died from shock and loss of blood. This method of execution, referred to as stacung or 'stanging', derives from the Norse word for 'pole' or stick with two sharp points attached for penetrating and breaking up the soil. Hardly identical to a pitchfork, the stang is listed among the appliances flown by witches to their Sabbat along with besoms, distaffs and goats. Some witches identified the stang as the Horned God although – in a notable iconic flourish – Grant Wood nailed it to the Puritan mast in *American Gothic*.

Bearing this in mind, let us recall what James Hayward said in 1875 after killing Ann for turning the evil eye on him and causing deaths of cattle. He had been "bewitched" all day and witches were in the glass of water he was given. "There are sixteen witches in Long Compton," he declared in his confession, "and if I had my way, I would kill them all. If you knew the number of people who lie in our churchyard, who, if it had not been for them, would have been alive now, you would be surprised. Her was a proper witch. I pinned Ann Tennant to the ground before slashing her throat with a billhook in the form of a cross."

The coroner, T.B. Couchman, ruled: "Wilful Murder, Deliberately Stabbed to Death by James Hayward with a Pitchfork under the Delusion of Witchcraft."

In view of the likeness between Ann Tennant's and Charles Walton's violent endings, the investigation took a slant that it would not have if there had been more witnesses and reliable evidence.

The idea was floated that Walton was slain in a sacrificial manner because Alfred Potter or someone else believed he was a witch who had cursed his cattle and brought a blight on his crops. This was not a proposition the police were happy to pursue, but they had little choice. Without names and details, it invited the possibility of ridicule, and they wanted to be regarded as a modern, efficient force, not as a team of buffoons caught up in a medieval whodunnit. But as other motives had so far proven resistant, they found themselves forced to consider the 'black arts'.

American Gothic by Grant Wood.

Professor J.M. Webster, forensic scientist

(Above) Body of Charles Walton

(Left) Professor J.M. Webster, the distinguished pathologist.

MEON HILL & THE ROLLRIGHTS

If the manner of Walton's death stirred echoes of witchcraft, the location was similarly meaningful. In his book, *Folk Lore, Old Customs and Superstitions in Shakespeare Land* (1929), J. Harvey Bloom recalls how in 1912 he could only get people in the neighbourhood to tell him stories about witches "with much persuasion and some fear of the consequences." He quotes a local proverb: "There are enough witches in Long Compton to draw a wagon-load of hay up Long Compton hill." Meon Hill is classed as a "witch district" where the Wild Hunt may be seen stampeding across the fields:

Among the villages of the plain below the hill are many old folk living to tell those they can trust creepy stories of the Hell-hounds, Night-hounds, or Hooter, as they are variously named, that in phantom wise, with hounds and horn, pursue phantom foxes along the hill-tops at midnight. Many are the legends to account for uncouth sounds at night, which certainly do occur. One story is told of a local huntsman who would not desist from his favourite sport even on the Sabbath. On one Sunday judgement fell upon the ungodly crew, huntsmen, horses and hounds fell into a chasm that opened in the hill and were never seen again, though they still in ghostly wise hunt at midnight.

Meon Hill has earthworks on it from which Bronze Age relics have been recovered. In earlier times a "wake" or all-night fair was held there. There is a legend of it being made by the Devil.

In a fit of annoyance at seeing Evesham Abbey built, he kicked a clod of earth at it, but a saint's prayer deflected it: hence the clod fell short forming Meon Hill. Legends of things being "made by the Devil" are common throughout the British Isles and may indicate a former pagan landmark.

If the police were prepared to accept the historic provenance of 'stanging' or impaling, along with the folklore and superstition attached to Meon Hill, there was a yet another matter worthy of looking into – namely the time of Charles Walton's death?

If the date, February 14th, *was* intentional, it would seem flagrantly inappropriate. Why select St Valentine's Day – associated with flirtation and amorous dalliance – for a crime of such savagery? Romantic associations aside, February is a month of blight and extinction, the time of the Ice Moon, when the vegetation is dead, the trees black and denuded, each bough stiff-clenched and in thrall to the Lord of Winter. The name derives from 'Februa', the Roman 'Festival of Purification' or cleansing by way of sacrifice. It was also the time of the Lupercalia, derived from Lupercus, god of shepherds whose priests wore goatskins after the manner of the Greek priests of Pan. In the Lupercal, the cave where Romulus and Remus were suckled by a she-wolf, there was a statue of the god. On the Ides of February, a goat and a dog were sacrificed there, and salt mealcakes prepared by Vestal Virgins.

The whereabouts of Hayward's attack on Ann Tennant struck many as portentous, near the ancient circle of the Rollright Stones, twelve miles from Meon Hill. This alliance stretches commonsense, for Ann and James, being natives of Long Compton, dwelt in the vicinity of the stones. Therefore *anything* they did, however commonplace, could be related to the monument. Nevertheless, for those who style James's assault as a sacrificial gesture, the Rollrights supply an apt context, drawing in a host of pagan associations. Like other famous megaliths, they are invoked alongside Albion's original priesthood, the Druids, who also bring with them murky rumours of the sacrifices they were alleged to perform at moonset, sunset or equinoctial quarter.

Set high up on a plateau, the circle is a bracing and fascinating site. The stones form a complicated grouping, stooping and bristly like a conclave of magical beings out of *Lord of the Rings*. The King's Stone and The Whispering Knights stand apart and aloof. Wonderfully honeycombed, the latter take their name from the conspiratorial way in which they huddle together like a megalithic family.

Britain's Druid population was massacred in AD 61 by the army of Suetonius Paulinus on their last stronghold, the Isle of Anglesey, leaving the singularly despised figure of the witch to deputise for Britain's pagan forefathers.

47

In the swampy wastes of popular historical knowledge – an oozy tangle of lore, legend and fact – the witch glimmers and entices, from the slithery, alluring enchantress Morgan Le Fay to the "black and midnight hags" of Shakespeare's *Macbeth*.

In the context of the Rollrights and the Cotswolds, they firmly belong with many a local yarn citing their escapades, sayings, herbs, cures and curses. Shakespeare, himself from Stratford-upon-Avon, has one of his characters say, "Blood will I draw on thee, thou art a witch!"

Legends of witches attach themselves to the stones as well as local fertility rites. The best known tells of a King who wanted to conquer all of England. On reaching the Rollrights, he was confronted by a witch who challenged him with these words:

"Seven long strides shalt thou take
And if Long Compton thou canst see,
King of England thou shalt be."

The King took up the challenge, striding to attain the view of Long Compton, but was obstructed by a long mound known as the Arch-Druid's barrow. The witch mocked him. Having failed the test, she stated that he would not be King of England but instead he and his men would be turned into stone while she would take on the guise of an elder. Hence the King became the King's Stone, his men the King's Men Stone Circle, and his knights the Whispering Knights.

Another legend says that on New Year's Eve, at the tolling of the bells of Long Compton church, the stones go down to the valley to drink. In addition girls who harboured doubts about their fertility would go out at midnight and press their breasts against the megaliths, a ritual also observed by French peasant women at Carnac.

In an article in *Folk-Lore* (1895), Arthur J. Evans writes of "a great cave beneath the King Stone, and according to some the same exists beneath the circle too." This same opening leads to the realm of the fairy folk who are said to live beneath the circle in great caverns, some of which are linked up to the monolith across the road.

A 'Witches Sabbat' was reportedly observed here, 12 May 1949, by a woman who saw shadowy figures, male and female, dancing "in a queer fashion and bouncing up and down as if they were on pogo sticks…"

Another witness, Mr J.F. Rogers of Banbury, watched from behind one of the stones. "There was more mumbling than any talking or singing," he said, "and I couldn't hear a word. When they were still, the leader made some signs and gestures and stood by the King's Stone. He had some kind of disguise – I could have sworn it was a goat's mask or something."

More recently, a sensitive called Alex Peach spent a night in a field near the Stones only to be rudely awakened at 2 am by loud growls and grinding roars. He opened his eyes to the glare of dazzling headlights that made him shrivel in terror. Two tractors were tearing down on him – a drunken farmer and his sons were holding some sort of gladiatorial contest with their vehicles. Fearing being trampled into the soil like a cabbage, he ran from the spot screaming.

HONORARY WITCH CONSULTANT

Margaret Murray

Because of a lack of obvious leads, the Egyptologist and expert on witchcraft, Margaret Murray, was invited to comment on the murder of Charles Walton, both to the police and the press. An amazing, limber old lady, bright-eyed and shrewd as a weasel, she was over eighty in 1945 and starting to look deliciously barmy. There are marvellous shots of her with an ear trumpet – how well she would have looked as a batty victim in *Kind Hearts and Coronets* or playing the part of Frank Baker's *Miss Hargreaves*. A brilliant if erratic scholar, she produced several controversial books on witchcraft, notably *The Witch-Cult in Western Europe* (1921), locating the origins of witchcraft in early Paleolithic fertility cults, and *The God of the Witches* (1931), dealing with the genesis of the male horned god, and the stupendously audacious *The Divine King in England*, arguing that several notable historical deaths – including those of Joan of Arc and King Rufus in the New Forest – were ritual acts.

In *The God of the Witches*, she classed witchcraft as the oldest nature religion, dating back to Neolithic times. The chief deity of the cult was the Horned God, later corrupted into the image of the biblical Satan. Contemporary specialists allow witches a less extensive lineage. Ronald Hutton dates their faith five years *after* the Walton Murder when honorary warlock, Gerald Gardner, started putting it together, inviting Aleister Crowley to lend a hand in the enterprise. Hutton, a respected historian and Britain's foremost academic on matters of folklore, festival and Druidry, undoubtedly knows his broomsticks – for he is an honourable pagan himself. What, of course, he means is that no *structured religion* of witchcraft existed before Gardner arrived on the scene.

But there may well have been 'witches' in rural villages and hamlets (if the term may be applied to men and women who gathered herbs, mixed potions for healing and dabbled in astrology). The notion of the 'Witches Sabbat', where they gathered to honour Satan, was likely a fantasy invented by priests and prosecutors during the great witch hunts of medieval Europe. Rooting out and burning heretics became a cottage industry, offering work to carpenters, demonologists and food-vendors who sold pies and snacks during the holocausts and hangings. When the commotion died, many lost their livelihood, as in the banning of fox-hunting today. Nearly all the gruesome associations arise from the accuser or lawyer specifically outlining the scenario that had been branded his imagination. Picture him flourishing a pair of hot tongs and bawling: "Confess you assembled on Lark Hill at midnight, that you kissed the buttocks of the Devil and afterward vomited a stream of toads. Confess! Confess!"

The victim would only have to let out a gasp of assent and sign a bit of bloody paper and the torturer had extracted a full confession. If the witch had not been sighted near the place of her alleged felony, a hare or raven appearing in the same spot would serve equally well, as it was accepted they could shape-shift at will. One pragmatic, level-headed English magistrate protested at justice being warped in such a way, saying: "This is utter nonsense. Do you not think, if this poor old woman indeed had the power to change into a bird, she'd not do so now and fly away from these foolish, fantastical accusations?"

On the larger issue of the provenance of witchcraft, if there had been an organised female cult during the Middle Ages and later, congregating on hilltops for midnight orgies with the Devil, one might have expected to find descriptions of their revels from the thousands of shepherds all over Europe, so it is rather odd that only the persecutors flourished the evidence. This lack of historic precedent prompted Hutton to dub 'Wicca' as the modern religion Britain has given to the world. This is true in the sense that Gerald Gardner consciously and artfully put it together around 1950. Naturally Hutton would concede witches were around hundreds of years back, but they were not a religion so much as a scatter of country folk who still used traditional techniques for wishing well and ill and looking into the future.

But back in 1945, at the time of the Lower Quinton murder, Margaret Murray was *the* single widely acknowledged spokeswoman on witchcraft. She saw it as a remnant of the original faith of the British Isles, revolving around nature worship and the horned god. Once prevalent, it was now only patchily active in rural locales. Her notion had a persuasive clarity that impressed antiquarians and folklorists. Hence the historicity of the 'Old Religion', perpetuated in folk festival and superstition, achieved a fairly wide credence. The idea of witches worshipping in their traditional way in secret locations in the British Isles was attractive to those who liked a pinch of sensation in their lives. It made the cult appear more secure and palpable than it was. Hence people started to seek out witches where none were hiding, and Margaret Murray took the lead in all this hoary speculation and jittery revisionism.

So when Fabian's routine interrogations failed to yield clues, he invited Margaret, who was Britain's most famous witchcraft scholar, to comment on their findings. This resulted in her spending a weekend at Lower Quinton. Taking with her an artist's sketch book, she dropped in on the village fête, talked to locals and told children fairy stories. Colonel Geoffrey White, Chief Constable of Warwickshire, invited her to examine the police dossier and photographs relating to the murder. Subsequently her views were printed in the *Birmingham Post*:

I think there are still remnants of witchcraft in isolated parts of Great Britain and I believe that Charles Walton was one of the people sacrificed. I think this because of the peculiar way in which he had been killed. His throat had been cut and a pitch-fork had been used after he was dead to prevent him being moved. The sacrifices are carried out by people who still believe in a religion practised in Britain before Christianity who we call devil-worshippers. They still work Black Magic. The belief is that if life is taken out of the ground it must be replaced by a blood sacrifice. I am not interested in the murder, only in the witches. I think it was a murder without normal motive – no money was missing and there was no other reason why the old man should have been killed.

Belief in witchcraft had not rendered Margaret over-credulous as to its efficacy. "Witches cannot do anything supernatural," she emphasised in a later article in the *Sunday Dispatch*. "It is the belief of people around them that makes them witches. In other words, if there were no people to believe in them, there would be no witches. If, for instance, anyone cursed by a witch just laughed it off and refused to take it seriously, it would have no efficacy at all. Witches, therefore, are individuals who are believed by those around them to have certain unusual powers, either for good or evil. Other people believe them to be witches and in some rural areas even to this day, once that reputation has been acquired, it sticks."

Several years later (June 1956) she was still writing on the murder, paying attention to the date of the operation:

There was also the significance of the day—the 14th of February. In pre-Christian times February was a sacrificial month, when the soil was spring-cleaned of the dirt of winter. In the old calendar February 2nd was a sacrificial day, but the old calendar was 12 days behind ours, which means that February 14th corresponds to February 2nd. But I found nothing to support my theory beyond that. The pitchfork was never an instrument of sacrifice in this country, though it may have been in Italy—and there were Italian prisoners-of-war in the neighbourhood at the time.

Despite a surface scepticism, Margaret did not mind giving it a whiz. From time to time, she tried out witchery – for instance, casting spells in a saucepan and trying to topple academic appointments of which she disapproved. This was not unlike Jung's animism, talking to his kitchen utensils in his tower in Bollingen, believing they'd provide better dishes if personally cultivated. Such activities were partly playful on her part, for she could be witty and astute even into late old age, remarking to Leonard Cottrell in a BBC broadcast she made at the age of ninety-six: 'I've been an archaeologist most of my life and now I'm a piece of archaeology myself.'

Another so-called expert on these matters saw the murder in terms of a witch taking revenge on a fellow practitioner:

It is almost certain that the murderer is a landowner, or the owner of cattle or sheep. Quite possibly he mistook a harmless 'white' witch, which is what the murdered man may well have been, for a black witch. White witchcraft involves harmless rites of fertility, but they could be mistaken for curses on crops and cattle. A friend of mine in this part of Warwickshire tells me that local gossip points to an 'evil eye' killing because there have been many curious incidents during this past spring. There was the unaccountable death of a heifer in a ditch which the veterinary surgeon could not explain. And he also said it was quite unknown for crops to be so bad when the weather has been so good. This has, not unnaturally in a rural community, given rise to superstitious talk of the actions of a 'black witch'.

The writer goes on to cite the instance of the Scottish witch, Isobel Gowdie, who was allegedly initiated by the Devil or a demonic deputy in her parish church. At the time of her trial confession, May 1662, she stated that she and other members of the coven had put spells on the land of their enemies, blighting and depriving them of their crops. She had made thistles grow where corn normally arose and had constructed a toy plough with traces made of dog-grass and a ram's horn. The tiny construction was yoked to toads who drew it across the ground to the accompaniment of the witches chanting implorations to make the land sterile.

The King's Stone, the most isolated of the Rollrights.

BLACK DOG

S ince the prolonged investigation, Fabian noted in a report at the end of April how the affairs of Alfred John Potter were faltering. Charles Henry Batchelor was no longer the carefree 'Happy' who pulped mangolds on the day of the murder. He had given Potter his notice – apparently over a wages disagreement. The farmer had turned down his request for a rise, he told Fabian, so he had left and acquired work elsewhere. But the Chief Inspector sensed Batchelor was also "prompted to leave by suspicions he may have formed regarding his former employer's connection with the death of Charles Walton."

Another employee of Potter's, John Workman, gave up his job at The Firs after the murder. His demeanour suggested to Fabian that he too suspected Potter had a played a role in Charles Walton's death.

Fabian and his assistant, Sergeant Webb, together with Warwickshire's chief detective, Alex Spooner, had been seeking further clues, but they never manifested. Unfortunately the crime scene had been hopelessly trampled by the search party and the local constabulary had removed the body without marking the location and conditions. Despite these oversights, Fabian made it his strategy to revisit it whenever the situation was desperate and devoid of leads.

In the case of Charles Walton, with only Potter as a viable witness, these persistent re-examinations turned out fruitless.

Nor did the attitude of the locals give him much cause for hope. "The natives of Upper and Lower Quinton," he observed, "and the surrounding district are of a secretive disposition and they do not take easily to strangers. Therefore I have borne in mind the possibility of there being some local history attached to the murdered man or his neighbours which we have not yet touched upon and which may have a direct bearing on the murder. The local police officers are keeping in close touch with the inhabitants of the district in the hope of bringing to light any such matter as would open a fresh line of enquiry. If, as I believe, this murder was committed by a local person, I do not think it possible for the matter to end without there being some repercussion which will give rise to an opportunity for us to take such action as may solve the mystery and bring the murderer to justice."

Despite this constructive forecast, Fabian was basically conceding defeat. After conducting over two thousands interviews and taking numerous samples of blood, skin and hair, he felt none the wiser. Stonewalled by locals, frustrated by suspects who offered such a paucity of useful testimony that he might as well have not taken them in for questioning, probably for the first time in what had been a phenomenally successful career he was confronting failure. "When Albert Webb and I walked into the village pubs," he wrote in his memoir *The Anatomy of Crime*, "silence fell like a physical blow. Cottage doors were shut in our faces and even the most innocent witnesses seemed unable to meet our eyes."

Why were the natives of Lower Quinton so tight-lipped and reserved? Why did they not speak about their neighbours in an easy, colloquial way? Of course, it may not have been that they were resentful or desirous of thwarting the police, but simply had not the slightest idea who would enact such a horrific assault on Old Charlie, and now, what with this bizarre witchcraft angle, they were aghast.

Even today, many feel uneasy with the occult, and it must have been singularly disquieting for the wartime residents of Lower Quinton to one day be living in a serene, deep-thatched Cotswold Village, and the next finding it transformed into a haunt of witches and warlocks, a village of the damned, bedevilled by wicked rumours and stern-eyed cops striding from house to house, asking whether they might happen to know of any crazed, pitchfork-wielding neighbour capable of directing a maniacal battering against a frail, elderly man. Surely news of this kind would not enhance their social profile or increase the market value of their properties? No wonder many insisted the murderer could not have been a local.

To the police, it must have been singularly frustrating, trying to maintain a practical enquiry, seeking clues that would lead towards closure or solution, but instead being befuddled by dubious learning, hearsay and supernatural lore – miscellanea that possessed an uncanny fascination but did not advance the investigation or narrow it to a point of guilt. No, what these echoes from the past did was *block* the way through. Contemplating a present felony mirrored by a historical precedent is like setting up facing mirrors – what you got was not a solution but an inanity of replication. Simply there were too many signs and wonders and not enough ordinary clues.

One detail the police overlooked was the shadowy possibility of Ann Tennant being Charles Walton's great-grandmother. His great-grandparents were Thomas Walton and Ann Smith. The latter name was also the maiden name of Ann Tennant who was born in 1794. The speculation goes that she might have married Thomas Walton in January 1812, given birth to the victim's grandfather, William Walton, in 1814, and later marrying her second husband, John Tennant, April 1819.

AT THE GAY DOG

As a result of lack of leads, the perceptions of the police became rather more desperate than they might have otherwise.

One notable example occurred at dusk. Fabian was walking along the slope of Meon Hill when a black dog dashed past him. A few moments later, a young boy came traipsing up behind.

"Are you looking for your dog?" Fabian asked the child.

"What dog?" the boy asked.

Fabian said later that he noticed that the dog had vanished and the boy fled down the hill in terror.

According to Donald McCormick's colourful version of events, later that night Fabian entered the Gay Dog Inn, asking the locals if they knew anything about black dogs in the district, and whether they triggered anxiety.

One of the company responded with an illuminating monologue:

"Well, it's strange what you say and how you say it. I've never heard anyone actually claim to have seen that dog before, and yet there's a yarn about black dogs in these parts that's uncommonly like your story. We don't talk much about it – not since the war anyway. That's given us too much to talk about. And come to think of it, probably not since the last war, but I reckon long, long ago, there was a strange black dog around Quinton – a ghost dog you might call it. And the story goes this dog was seen nine nights in succession by a young farm lad on Meon Hill. Nothing specially remarkable in that, except that nobody knew where the dog came from and there was something mighty peculiar about the animal. It wasn't just that it was a large black dog, larger than most, but it was silent like and had a strange look about the eyes. Then, on the ninth night, by which time the boy had come to dread seeing it, the dog changed into a headless woman who glided past him, her black skirts swishing in the breeze. The boy felt there was some warning in this. And the next day his sister died."

Fabian left the pub but was unable to abandon the image of the black dog which seemed to pursue him, both as symbol and manifestation. Soon after, he heard a patrol car had ran over a dog in one of the twisting lanes near the village. It turned out to be a black dog, synonymous with death or tragedy. Later on, a black Labrador was found hanged by its collar on the branches of a bush on Meon Hill, not far from where Charles Walton's body had lain. It was a cruel and callous act – some might consider it an attempt to warn off the detectives.

While liaising with Inspector Hinksman of the Warwickshire Police Traffic Department, Fabian's attention was drawn to a reference in J. Harvey Bloom's book:

At Alveston a plough lad named Charles Walton met a black dog on his way home nine times in successive evenings. He told the shepherd and carter with whom he worked and was laughed at for his pains. On the ninth encounter a headless lady rustled past him in a silk dress, and on the next day he heard of his sister's death.

The obvious question: was this the same Charles Walton who was murdered?

Superintendent Spooner thought it was, telling Fabian it had happened on Meon Hill. As Charles Walton had spent most of his life in Lower Quinton and was known to everyone, the allusion to Alveston was probably a misplaced reference. If true, this provided a different perspective on Walton's life and reputation. Instead of being an obscure old man, he had been locally marked as a 'character', an oddball who had entered the pages of a literary work. He was akin to a 'cunning man' or seer who saw creatures from the otherworld and was maybe able to cast spells or "put the evil eye" on anyone who crossed him. If he enjoyed such a surreptitious reputation, then fear or hatred would be a logical motive for removing him. Hence the murderer would be a person who, quite literally, would "not suffer a witch to live."

When he tried to incorporate this angle in his enquiries, Fabian stated the folk in Lower Quinton changed from coldly indifferent to bluntly unhelpful. "It was like the pulling down of a shutter," he said. Some merely slammed the door or remarked on a season of poor crops and the death of a heifer – as if these related to Old Charlie's end.

But even here one has to be wary of Fabian's reportage. He may be 'covering' for his own failure to advance the case, hinting everyone in Lower Quinton was against him when they may have been as devoid of answers as he was. So, in a sense, in his later, popular comments on the murder rather than his severely rational 'special reports' for Scotland Yard, he helped stir the rumour that Charles Walton was the victim of a witch-cult. He had been dispatched in that way for putting the 'evil eye' on cattle and crops.

This angle was taken up by the sensation-hungry press, but it was a nebulous concept on which to base an enquiry. What exactly is a witch? Someone who worships the Old Dark Gods? Someone who knows about herbs, potions, spells, stars, correspondences, talismans, love charms and so on? From a policeman's angle, it was a bad thing to be diverted by such Gothic warpaint? A murderer's motives are nearly always bound up with jealousy, greed, hate or something equally unmystical – whether the victim be a witch or no. The main thing was to keep one's eye on the ball, but the problem was it had ceased to roll in a definite direction and Fabian and his men found themselves sinking with the body of Old Charlie into an occult mire.

Once the Devil enters any arena of human activity, he tends to leave a slimy trail of dead-ends and non-sequiturs. What he's best at is getting into people's heads, working them up and muddling their thoughts, for which the only cure is perhaps reading large chunks of David Hume.

Hence, on pursuing this left-hand path, the police encountered many a Gothic yarn and twisted tale, but nothing remotely enlightening.

The situation has not changed. Even today, the Devil wastes thousands of hours of police time and costs the British taxpayer millions (especially when he enters the mind of social workers in satanic abuse cases). Being a metaphysical or legendary construct, he does not coordinate with crime detection and serves justice poorly. When the obvious solution failed to yield clues, Fabian plunged into "the black tide of mud" (as Freud referred to occultism) to find out what lay beneath.

Not a lot, it seemed. The police were treated to anecdotes, learned and barmy, relating to orgies, curses and men and women writhing unashamedly before black-candled altars – a bubbling, sulphurous potage, ideal for Sunday newspapers but useless for detection.

Towards the end of April 1945, after pursuing every nefarious nuance and diabolic diatribe, they found they had got no nearer and, rather than waste any more time, they arranged to return to London.

Fabian in his 'showbiz' role fraternising with Danny Kaye and Sid Field.

THE SÉANCE

E ven without the probings of Scotland Yard, the body of Charles Walton would not lie still. It had become enshrouded in rumours of witchcraft and ritual sacrifice and journalists appreciated to what extent a sensational story, with darkly melodramatic overtones, was capable of boosting their circulation, and, if sex and nudity came into it, that was all the better. If none were on hand, they were perfectly able to devise situations wherein it might be added or introduced.

For there is news that unfurls spontaneously and there is news that is prodded into action by those who want to make it onto the front page. Suffice to say, the aura surrounding the murder of Charles Walton excited the imagination of many who took an interest in occultism. The salacious aspect of witchcraft had proven a reliable journalistic angle, but yet another dimension, too, awaited exploration. This was the nebulous realm of Walton's aggrieved, disembodied spirit. Was he still earthbound and hovering in the aether? Realising the post-mortal potential of the shocking deed, psychic societies sought out mediums who were willing to contact the old man and hear his side of the story? Would he be able to name the killer and lay the mystery to rest?

In particular, a group of associate members of the Birmingham Psychic Research Society planned to visit Meon Hill on 2nd February, 1952, Candlemas Day, to see if they might pick up a message or evidence relevant to the murder. Even though the day out was breathlessly anticipated, it had to be cancelled – for no psychic appeared to be up to the job. Obviously the macabre nature of the crime was a source of anxiety. Mediums did not want to engage with a spirit who had ended in such a dreadful way, frightened that the negative energy might possess them in an unseemly manner.

So nothing happened on that occasion. But once an idea has been floated, it will inevitably body forth into a full-blown event. Sooner or later, a psychic was bound to knock up Charles Walton.

The first attempt was made through a parish councillor of Moreton Murrell, Warwickshire, called Tony Mills, who had been deeply affected by the murder and the diabolic rumours it generated.

Founder-president of the Staffordshire Metaphysical Society, Mr Mills was determined to spiritually probe the case. After many setbacks and frustrations, he established an alliance with the Birmingham Psychic Society, asking if they could find a sensitive willing to query the mystery of Walton's demise. They selected a lady medium who agreed to accompany Mr Mills's group on their expedition to Meon Hill, 27th November.

It was a grimly oppressive day, with barely a leak of sunlight, when the party set off, arriving in blinding blizzard and dense darkness at Lower Quinton. A total of sixteen members, accompanied by a reporter from the *Birmingham Post*, made their way round the village and up the slope of Meon Hill:

Shortly after we started a blizzard began and sleet fell. At length baffled by the darkness of the night, Mr Mills could not find the exact spot where the murder was committed. The other members of the party, knowing they were in a short distance of it, decided to hold their séance at the point they had reached.

The medium, Mrs Hickinbottam of Birmingham, went into a trance and appeared to be speaking of a man named Walton. She pronounced: "I forgive, I forgive. I deserved what was coming to me, but not in such a brutal way."

After about ten minutes and some intelligible words, the medium came round supported by her friends to prevent her falling.

Meanwhile Mr Mills had found the white gate by which the body was found, not fifty yards from the gnarled willow tree. When the medium was told by him how near she was to the actual spot, she remarked: "The blow was struck by the tree."

After informing them fully of the established facts, it was time for the party to trudge back home.

"I must say," Mr Mills commented, "that in my subsequent research into the Walton Murder, I had an uncanny sense of evil. For instance I took a sample of the soil from the ground where Walton was murdered. I had it analysed and it was ordinary enough. But from the day on which I brought that ordinary bottle into my home – I was then living at Moreton Murrell – I had an extraordinary run of misfortune. My little girl took pneumonia three times in succession. I broke my ankle. Of my sixty chickens forty-five died unexpectedly and inexplicably. The cattle sickened and so on.

Of course I had considered the possibility of the soil being the malignant influence, but it seemed too absurd for words. Nevertheless the day I took the bottle and hurled it far away as I could, these odd mishaps stopped."

Becoming almost indignantly aware that all the information the spirit world had proffered corresponded with what was already known and established – not adding a crumb of original insight – Mr Mills continued to entrench his position, claiming the medium had named a suspect and produced a remarkably accurate testimony: "Charles Walton was definitely up to something queer."

Daylight photographs of the corner of the field where Charles Walton was murdered were taken by the psychic society. There was one image alone that gave them cause for concern, showing a white marking in the shape of a hideous woman's face, set in the hedge above where Walton's body had lain.

"How do you explain that?" asked Mr Mills.

Archaeologist, Jacqui Wood, holding a piece of the witches' cauldron recovered from Saveock Water – (see p.114, The Witches of Saveock).

THE SECOND INVESTIGATION

" Blood of a newt and toad, spot of henbane, top up
with gin——— "

A problem with the Walton Murder is that it was subject to more than one investigation: the enquiry by Fabian in 1945 and a follow-up conducted mainly by newspapers some ten years later. Naturally, with the passing of time, the streams of evidence and conjecture mingle, becoming a single pool. But there was a difference, in that the information that arose from Fabian's original enquiry was bonier and more to the point than the floral speculation and invention that came later.

The second enquiry took place about four years after the repeal of the old Witchcraft Act (1951) and the passing of the Fraudulent Mediums Act, enabling 'witches' or psychics to practise their art or religion without breaking the law, but not by claiming special powers in order to deceive or extract money. Many Christians disliked the idea of what they considered a blasphemous pagan religion being legalised.

Newspapers tried their best to whip up a furore of sensational tales, usually featuring orgies in which naked female witches writhed before black candles and drank blood of animals. Many sensational and bold claims were made, notably that a clan of rich, distinguished people, including lawyers, clergymen, MPs and royalty, were practising occultists whom the newspapers in due course would name and shame.

But as top warlock of the day, Gerald Gardner, was quick to detect, the majority of the stories emanated from a single source: an anonymous frightened lady who, despite witnessing cruelty, perversion and terror tactics, preferred to sell her stories to newspapers rather than provide the police with hard facts. Inevitably a great deal of murky smoke was raised in which it was difficult to detect a spark of truth.

When the Walton Murder was re-investigated by authors and journalists, they visited Lower Quinton and interviewed people who knew, or claimed to have known, Charles Walton. Nearly all failed to point out that, in the intervening decade, most of the so-called witnesses had read the sensational articles in the press and become overly witch-conscious or witch-obsessed. This resulted in Charles Walton being transformed from a modest, elderly countryman into a warlock and seer, knowing of charms, spells and possessing supernatural skills. How accurate are these accounts? His niece Edie never produced any information regarding his occult prowess, so are these additional insights, including the story reported by McCormick that he harnessed toads to a miniature plough like Isobel Gowdie, to be trusted? There is an all-too-human tendency for hindsight to become entwined with flocculent speculation.

A counter view might assess the second wave of evidence as the upshot of a franker, more objective examination, when things had quietened and people were better able to speak out frankly on these dark matters. But unfortunately what was added later did not relate to Charles Walton and his milieu so much as increase the tonnage of diabolic speculation under which it was already tottering.

Inevitably, when running a feature on the case, journalists preferred a melodramatic approach. On Sunday, 19th February, 1956, appeared the headline: *Black Magic Killer-Woman Talks*:

A terrified woman, driven grey-haired by some of the most evil men in Britain, offered last night to help solve the murder of Charles Walton, who was impaled with a pitchfork in a lonely Warwickshire field on St. Valentine's Day, 1945. She will give the name of the alleged murderer to Det. Supt. A. W. Spooner, Chief of the Warwickshire C.I.D. This woman, who begged me not to reveal her name, has offered to tell Det. Supt. Spooner everything – provided she is protected from the vengeance of Britain's black magic cults. For twelve frightful years she took part with other members of the cults in grotesque rites that stem from Britain's mysterious past. Now she wants the police to stamp out these evil practices. And she wants them to solve the 11-year-old crime she claims was a ritual murder.

The account goes on to described how, through the machinations of her husband, Peter Jackson, the lady was made attend 'religious' meetings in London and Birmingham where various repulsive rites were enacted. The latter frightened her so much that she dared not go to the police for fear of reprisal. If anyone tried to break away, the leaders of the cult threatened to scar their head with a knife.

Charles Walton's murderer, she said, was named by the Midlands leader of the cult who was ambitious. He had a plan to get 'Number One' in London' out of the way, so that he could gain national control himself. The paper went on to state the old man was sacrificed in manner identical to that of the killing of a woman in 1875 in nearby Long Compton. A woman was brought by car to the Cotswolds from a different part of the country to do the deed. In other words, it repeated a story in circulation since Fabian's enquiry, the main difference being a group of suspects were vaguely identified.

As Gerald Gardner noted in *The Meaning of Witchcraft*, it was "strange that it was this paper and not the lady herself, who gave this information to the police. They, of course, realised that they were legally bound to do so; but it seems very odd to me that anyone possessing such information, if it were genuine, should not have taken it straight to the authorities."

The next day, February 20th, 1956, further details were printed under the headline: *Murder at Black Mass, says Woman:*

A woman has come forward to say that a shepherd, killed eleven years ago, was murdered by a woman during a Black Mass at midnight. She says that she was once a member of a black magic society and that she knows the name of the killer. The body of the shepherd, 74-year-old Charles Walton, was found on St. Valentine's day, 1945, in the middle of a circle of stones in a field at Lower Quinton, Warwickshire. He had been killed by blows from a farm billhook and staked to the ground with a pitchfork. His neck was slashed in the shape of a cross. Villagers said it was a ritual murder. There was a similar murder on St Valentine's Day, 1875, at Long Compton, also in Warwickshire. The accuser, an elderly woman from Birmingham, will probably be interviewed by police this week.

However, in a later report in another paper, March 15th, 1956, the same informant told a different version of the Black Magic Murder. Their reporter had found her in a suburb of Wolverhampton, an attractive woman with haunted eyes:

Thirteen people took part in the ceremony. One of them knew Walton. The rest came from various parts of the country.

Walton was hedging that day in a field well away from houses and the road. The person who knew him approached him with two others. He was struck down. It was exactly midday.

Rapidly they mutilated his body, soaked some robes in his blood, drove in the pitchfork, and danced round the body.

Commenting on this, Gerald Gardner tried to achieve fair play on behalf of those who wished to follow the witch cult without being branded as depraved devil-worshippers. "I should be greatly obliged," he remarked, "if anyone could explain to me how thirteen people could dance round the body of a man which according to the evidence given at the inquest by one of the three people who found it, was lying close against the hedge, in a bit of a ditch."

Naturally, after witnessing the killing, the lady was shocked and wished to disassociate herself from the type of people who behaved like that. So she attempted to break away from the circle of their influence:

Within a few days the circle of silence was put on my doorstep. It was made of twigs and graveyard chippings. It meant 'Keep Quiet'.

But I could not live with myself. I told one of the leaders that I would go to the police.

That night, on my way home, I was grabbed and scalped. They took a complete circle of hair and skin from my head, using a doctor's scalpel.

Gardner aptly commented:

Now, where have we heard something like this before? If we read on we shall soon see as Mrs X, who claimed to be a former High Priestess of the black magic cult, described some of the shocking rites performed by the Black Magic circle.

At almost every ceremony I attended… there was wild singing and dancing, drinking and sexual depravity. Animals were killed and their blood poured into goblets. The 'priests' prayed to the Devil for help.

The altar is a parody of a Christian altar. The cross is placed upside down in a glass of water and the candles on a slant, almost upside down. Newcomers are initiated by being forced to drink the warm blood of animals.

Then they all drink glasses of spirits and dance round the altar. These newcomers wear white robes, which are soaked in blood. They have to sign a pact in blood, giving their souls to the Devil.

"This description," Gardner observed, "is almost exactly the same as that given by the coloured lady in 1955; so also is the story of her being attacked in order to intimidate her into silence, only now the alleged attack, which, it will be remembered, in the original case consisted merely of having a piece of hair slashed off, and which, according to the paper's account at the time, *was testified by a police surgeon* as having produced abrasions, bruising and swelling, and left 'cut roots...on the left hand side area', is now described as a scalping, the removal of a complete circle of hair and skin, using a doctor's scalpel."

It was a pity Gardner was never given a fair hearing. He was a good writer with a quick eye and a sense of humour. He captured the farcical aspect of the Black Magic stories and proved a sharper sleuth than Fabian; for he was the first to catch on that the fiendish plague sweeping the nation, the swarms of young women presently in obeisance to Satan and the high-up individuals who regularly danced around black altars, were largely figments of the imagination of a single unstable lady who had found a secondary source of income in concocting such tales.

Few realised the "coloured lady" was a police 'informer' of sorts. This was a sensible move on her behalf, as the constabulary does not look kindly on those who sell features on lawbreakers rather than report them. Hence she did a bit of both. Let us now hear a little more about this virtuous observer of witchery: specifically the information and names – almost certainly through fear of libel – kept out of the reports. What follows is drawn from primary sources and provides the small print behind the block headlines.

The threatened lady's name was Mrs Shar-i-jay Jones who spoke Romany as well as English and was born in Spain. With her husband, Peter Jackson, she went to occult meetings in Birmingham held on the premises of the Heslaw Press. There she met Mr Unett, who was in charge, and several others who come over as inanely genteel rather than diabolical: "Dame Cadbury and Mrs Bell who took an interest in the Royal Family and the Mountbattens."

Curiously, Mrs Jones described 'Dr Gardner' as attending the meetings, meaning Gerald Gardner who later commented ironically on her adventures. As he had already received adverse press publicity for his ritual interests, she thought it apt to hallucinate his attendance along with other thrilling antics that he later read about with a mixture of bated breath and indignation, knowing such publicity would not help the formation of a new Wicca religion.

Mrs Jones tipped the journalist working on the *Sunday Pictorial*, Peter Hawkins, that the murder was carried out by a woman living in Cornwall who had been brought up to Stratford-upon-Avon for the task. This sounded fantastic to Hawkins, so he decided to vet the information. He checked up on the lady Mrs Jones identified. This was a Mrs Patricia McAlpine who lived at a house called Wheal Betsy near Newlyn, Cornwall. The police discreetly looked into the background of this lady "who had been seen going into a tunnel that led from her house into the sea" and discovered she was associated with the Great Beast, Aleister Crowley, briefly becoming his mistress and giving birth to his son, Ataturk, who was born in a hideout in Northumberland in 1937.

Later Patricia went to live in Scotland, giving birth to several and 'mothering' a total of seven children, three of whom returned to Wheal Betsy.

As I have examined this claim more extensively in a previous book *The Tregerthen Horror* (dealing with the death of Rupert Brooke's ex-mistress, Ka Cox, at a haunted cottage on Zennor Moor), I will not expand further, merely emphasise that Pat McAlpine or Pat Doherty, grand-daughter of the celebrated Newlyn painter, T.C. Gotch, although she enjoyed an exciting, fitfully hazardous life, did not perpetrate the Walton Murder, but the police did contact and interview her in the interests of thoroughness rather than high expectation.

Identifying the Walton Murder with Aleister Crowley was the kind of smouldering back-tracking that appealed to Sunday newspapers. For Crowley, at the time of the murder, lacked the litheness of limb or a convincing raison *d'être* to do such a deed, being an old man intent on setting his affairs in order.

Even journalists realised it was unlikely a dead ditcher would be of any use to a sophisticated occultist who confined his ceremonies to flats and hideouts in London, but such objections hardly mattered when millions awaited the latest dish of devilment.

(Left) Gerald Gardner, founder of Wicca – he thought Walton's death an attempt to avenge the 'evil eye'.

(Right) Patricia Doherty, mistress of Aleister Crowley & unlikely suspect in the Lower Quinton murder.

When Crowley died in 1947, Fabian attended his funeral, noting among the mourners leaders of covens in Lewes, Shoreham and London. He wanted to prosecute Satanists and witches but feared for the safety of his men: "Penetration of the deepest depths of witchcraft is achieved by a complicated six-month course of initiation... Intoxicated and hypnotised, even the most solid and hard-headed member of the force could succumb."

Surely Fabian's problem would not be infiltrating the network so much as pinpointing what was technically 'criminal' about their actions. By then, he was already succumbing to the allure of publicity. The previous year, 1946, he had visited George Bernard Shaw for his 90th birthday and secured the great writer's fingerprints. Vanity was taking hold, but he was able to adapt to demand, separating his dry, disciplined police work from the material suited to newspapers.

IN DEFENCE OF POTTER

Nearly every writer on the Walton Murder concludes by pointing an accusing finger at Alfred Potter. He remained Fabian's strongest suspect and McCormick, without actually naming, indicates Potter killed Charles Walton because he saw him as a witch who had caused sickness in his cattle.

Supernatural theorising aside, logical connections between Potter and the crime immediately suggest themselves:

1. When a murder takes place, usually perpetrator and victim know each other. A stormy relationship or argument may trigger the crime. Potter and Walton had an established working relationship and there was a rumour that Potter owed Walton money.

2. The murderer used the tools on hand to his advantage, cutting Walton's torso with the slash-hook and impaling him with the hayfork. This hints at an 'insider' logic that may well derive from prior acquaintance.

3. As if to allay his guilt and unease, Potter behaved suspiciously from the start. At the crime scene, he complained of cold and feeling unwell as if the horror of the murder of his trusted employee was secondary to his personal comfort. Worried that his fingerprints might be found on the murder weapons, he provided contradictory, confusing accounts of where he was and what he saw. He behaved like a man who was hiding something.

Using reductive logic, Fabian concluded Potter was most likely the killer, but he was far from certain, conceding:

Although the suspicions attaching to Potter will be well-appreciated, there is no real evidence to connect him with the murder itself, and no reasonable motive can be found for his committing it. The murder was of a particularly violent and brutal character and there is not the slightest evidence that Potter is of a violent disposition. Neither is there any suggestion that he and Walton had ever quarrelled.

Behind Potter's blunt, faltering replies, Fabian sensed much was hidden. Like others in Lower Quinton, Potter was compliant with the police, but did not open out, expand a point or enlighten. This was perplexing as, with a murderous fiend on the loose, locals should have been anxious to assist the cause of law and order.

72

In addition Fabian noted:

When interviewed Potter has always appeared morose and sullen and even when closely interrogated has never lost his temper or become other than respectful. He is unkempt and would appear, on the surface, to be dull-witted but I am convinced he is far from that. He is a man of considerable strength and, in my opinion, is an extremely cunning individual.

Again this sounds suspicious but being the police's chief suspect in a bloodthirsty murder is a morose, sullen situation. In his dealings with others, however, Fabian supplies evidence of Potter being amenable and civilised:

Several girls attached to the Women's Land Army who have been employed by Potter at Firs Farm from time to time have been seen but they can tell us nothing of interest. The statements of Margaret May Brooks, Lily Patricia Chance and Betty Rose Ivy Jeynes are attached. They all say that Potter was kind and considerate to them during their employment with him.

Not long before he died, Robert Fabian spoke to the historian of crime, Richard Whittington-Egan, on the murder, saying he was convinced Alfred Potter was the only person who could have done it. After all, he was the last to see Charlie alive and had been worried that his fingerprints might be left on the murder implements. He was able to find his way quickly to the body in the dark, and it was hinted that he owed Old Charlie money. His temper after drinking was said to be fractious – although no evidence to support of this has appeared – and his statements to the police were confusing and contradictory.

All this surely pointed to his guilt – save that many of the accusations could be given a sympathetic twist. He found his way quickly to the body because he knew his own fields like the back of his hand; he placed his fingers on the trouncing-hook or hayfork to try to remove it or shield Edie from the horror of seeing her uncle pinned down like that; his confusing manner with the police was because he was unnerved by the ferocity of the murder. As for Edie Walton telling Fabian of her uncle loaning money to Potter, if true, that was the product of hindsight, for there is no mention of it in her original testimony.

STATEMENT OF EDITH ISOBEL WALTON, 23rd February 1945:

"My Uncle Charles Walton never worked on a Saturday or on a Sunday. He never worked if it was wet or if there was too much wind. Neither did he work if there was fog, snow or ice on the road. I cannot remember when my uncle last worked a full week. During the winter he would work very few weeks – full weeks were very occasional. One time he stayed home a fortnight on a sick list. A doctor from Mickleton came to see him. My uncle always went up to fetch his money from Mr Potter on a Saturday. I wouldn't be sure if he went every week or once a fortnight. However, if my uncle only worked a few hours in a week, he wouldn't go and fetch his money on a Saturday but leave it until the following week. I never had any idea how much money he drew from Mr Potter and I never heard him talk of being short or having any difficulty with wages. I never heard my uncle say he'd lent any money to anyone and I never saw him with any IOUs. Either the last time or the time before that when my uncle went to see Mr Potter, Mr Potter killed two pigs. I think that was the last time, but I cannot be sure of it. I can't remember any Saturday when my uncle didn't go round to collect his money, except when he was ill in bed. His doctor was Doctor Van der Meyn of Mickleton. About 5.30 pm on 17th February 1945, I went to Stratford-upon-Avon mortuary and there identified the body of my uncle Charles Walton."

AN APPALLING, FOOLHARDY RISK

Potter was a family man and, middle-age crisis aside, it was unlikely he should turn into an atrocious killer mid-point in his career, making his stolid churchgoing wife an accessory in a gory tissue of lies and deceptions. Potter was 'said' to have a bad temper, especially after he'd been drinking, but the attack on Walton was a bestial rite that iced the blood of senior detectives. If Potter secreted such molten urges, how had he managed to suppress them until middle age? Most psychopaths express their natures earlier. If he *did* owe Walton money and the other was putting on the pressure, Edie might have had *some* idea. Neither was Potter impoverished. Alfred's father, Leonard, was an entrepreneur, buying in 1942 the handsome coaching inn, The Lygon Arms at Chipping Camden. The property passed to Alfred's son, Ivor – a popular local character.

But let us suppose Charlie Walton *was* demanding return of cash he had loaned. If he had not been wily enough to ratify the agreement by legal document or IOU, Potter would have no proven obligation to repay. He could claim he had been given the money. And surely, ailing old Charlie would not continue to work humbly for a pittance from a man who owed him a large amount?

Potter was close both to the victim and scene of crime. Through paucity of clue alone, the accusation sticks. If he had planned the murder, he must have known he'd be the obvious suspect, who would not only have to go through gruelling interviews with senior detectives, but also be questioned at the coroner's court and, should matters turn against him, be convicted of murder. Literally his life and reputation would be destroyed, so what had he got to gain? Also, such a hair-raising, blatant mode of assault, conducted in broad daylight, might have been anticipated as producing horrifically loud shrieks and screams, drawing people across the fields, so why take an appalling, foolhardy risk? Tess Kingham also noted (p 36) how Professor Webster's lengthy back calculation (10½ hours) from rigor mortis nudges Potter's 'alibi' period. The evidence is far from clear cut.

View of Lower Quinton fifty years ago.

Today Lower Quinton appears a prosperous, immaculately kept community, gently overshadowed by the bulk of Meon Hill that looms and spreads in wooded spurs and sloping fields. Black and white cottages, with rustic beams and interlocking timberwork – including Charles Walton's former home – emit a shipshape glow and the golden stone of the College Arms warmly reflects the sunlight. It is a rural idyll that bears not the faintest trace of barbaric or unnatural acts.

In order to prepare a feature on the murder, about seven years back, the BBC spoke to locals, including Mrs Wakelon at the village stores. "People don't talk about it," she said. "Those that would know about it are gone, except one who's in hospital and another that's in a nursing home." The lady who ran the village post office, Joyce, was similarly adamant. "No one will, talk to you about it... I have no answers to your questions."

When I had a drink at the College Arms, I sensed the locals' enquiring glances. People are quick to pick out writers and journalists, probably by the strained casualness of their furtive glances. I did not bring up the murder, knowing they were of another generation, prosperous retired people from Stratford, young farmers and their wives, upwardly mobile incomers. Many knew who Charles Walton was, but I doubted whether any could locate the site of the murder, let alone supply data. Why should they dwell on it? What light could they throw anymore than Whitechapel residents could identify Jack the Ripper? The Walton family had left, Farmer Potter's house was demolished, and the last person who recalled the original enquiry was dead.

I thought of Edward Arlington Robertson's villanelle:

They are all gone away,
The house is shut and still,
There is nothing more to say.

Through broken walls and gray
The winds blow bleak and shrill:
They are all gone away.

Nor is there one today
To speak them good or ill:
There is nothing more to say.　　　　　*(The House on the Hill)*

WHO KILLED BELLA?

Because they took place within two years of each other in the Midland area, were both shockingly brutal, inexplicably mysterious, with occult overtones and shared the same forensic expert, Professor Webster, it is usual to place the Lower Quinton and Hagley Wood murders together. Tess Kingham thought that they shared suspicious features, but sharply contrasted the attitudes of two police forces:

Interestingly the Warwickshire Police were more than helpful with any Walton material. However the force maintaining the Bella files were most definitely not. I was passed from pillar to post, obviously stalled, had to put a request in writing several times and no joy!

The tragic and startling 'Hagley Wood Murder' or 'Wych Elm Case' began on a sunny April day in 1943 on the outskirts of the conurbation of Birmingham. Four teenage boys, Bob Farmer, Bob Hart, Fred Payne and Tommy Willets from nearby Stourbridge, were roaming over the Clent Hills They entered Hagley Wood, hoping to find some birds' nests – a quest that led to an old, hollowed-out wych–hazel, also known as a Wych Elm, on account of its size and age.

While scrambling around the wizened hulk, one of them, Bob Farmer, let out a cry. A white skull was grinning at him from the tree. "There was a small patch of rotting flesh on the forehead," he recalled, "with lank hair attached to it, and the two front teeth were crooked."

The frightened boys ran. They had no idea if the skull was human or animal and did not spread the word. But Tommy Willets, the youngest, eventually confided to his father.

The information was passed to Sergeant Skerratt of Clent. He hurried to the spot and confirmed it was a human skull and took measurements. The hole in the tree was three feet six inches from the ground and about two feet in diameter at its widest.

Police reconstruction of Bella

NOTICEABLE IRREGULARITY FRONT TEETH, LOWER JAW

HEIGHT ABT. 5 FT.

BROWN HAIR

DARK BLUE STRIPED KNITTED WOOLLEN CARDIGAN

LIGHT BLUE BELT

AGE ABT. 35

MOCK WEDDING RING (VALUE 2/6)

CLOTH SKIRT WITH ZIP

PEACH COLOURED TAFFETA UNDER SKIRT

BLUE, CREPE SOLED SHOES

Tommy Willets who found 'Bella'

The tree was 125 yards from the Birmingham road, near a narrow lane by the side of the wood. Sergeant Skerratt, suspecting foul play, placed a guard on the tree and the next morning, 19th April 1943, Professor J.M. Webster, Superintendent Sidney Inight and Detective Inspector Tom Williams checked the scene.

In the tree stump was not only found a skull with bits of flesh clinging to it but a shoulder blade, a spinal column, a few ribs, a shoe and bits of decayed clothing that had no labels or identity markers. A gold wedding-ring and some crêpe shoes were found lying nearby. What was alarming was that the right hand was missing. They found it later intact about thirteen paces from the tree. The bones were taken away and analysed by Professor Webster (who later presided over the autopsy of Charles Walton). They made up the skeleton of a woman whose body had been forced inside the tree with a bunch of taffeta rammed into her mouth, giving rise to the coroner's verdict "murder by asphyxiation by some person or persons unknown." [4]

Professor James Webster reported she was around 35, had previously given birth to a child and been dead for about 18 months before she was found. A massive police enquiry was set in motion, examining over 3000 reports of missing women within a 1000-mile radius. Local and national records were searched, including dental charts and medical records.

Even the maker of her crêpe-soled shoes was traced and a list of customers and trading contacts, but that yielded nothing. Nor did a search of dental records – usually a sure sign of identity – find a match with the irregular teeth of her low jaw. Her clothing, dark blue striped knitted cardigan, cloth skirt and light blue belt, was not expensive and her height that of a child, only five feet tall (before the Second World War, people tended to be more varied in height and shape). Bella also wore a cheap mock wedding-ring, worth about 2/6d, a rather pathetic touch that hardly hints at her being well-educated or well-to-do.

Because no one knew who she was, it was thought unlikely she was local, possibly a refugee. The bombing of the major industrial centres had driven people out of the great conurbations. Many moved in with their relatives in the countryside or walked out on their old lives in search of somewhere safer. Mindful of the crisis, the hospitable village of Hagley, outside Birmingham, took in evacuated mothers and their children in addition to staff of the workforce from RAF Hartlebury while nearby Pedmore was billeting part of the Welsh Regiment. This was during nights of total blackout when violent deeds

---

[4] The verdict has been questioned because Bob Farmer, who picked up the skull, wedged bits of rotten fabric in the jaws, so that the stick he used would hold in place as he prodded it back into the tree.

might go unseen and some police officers thought two homeless people – one of a murderous disposition – came together in that lonely place with tragic consequences.

In addition there were foreigners, Jews, Slovaks and Poles, who sought sanctuary, so it was a time of incessant mobility when it could prove difficult to trace a single person's movements. What with soldiers being posted to various camps, taking leave and then returning to duty, the police had to keep up with an ever-changing state of affairs in which it was relatively easy for an individual to slip through the net of surveillance.

After a revisit by the police to the scene of the crime, a clue appeared – an identity card was found lying under a bush near the tree-stump. It belonged to a woman who was traced to an address in the Midlands. The police called and asked her name. When she replied, they asked her to confirm her statement by showing her identity card.

"Certainly," she said and reached for her handbag, but could not find the card.

The police told her they had recovered it from Hagley Wood. How had it come to be there?

"I've no idea," the woman replied, "I've never been to Hagley Wood."

The police probed but no further explanation was forthcoming. She seemed to have no idea how anyone could have come by her card or taken it to Hagley Wood. They sought local people who had noticed things unusual. An executive of an industrial company came forward, saying that, in July 1941, he had heard a woman's screams coming from Hagley Wood while walking to his nearby lodgings. Not long after, he met a schoolteacher walking in the opposite direction who also confirmed the screams. The men phoned the police who searched Hagley Wood, but found nothing. This incident was dated 20 months before the corpse was brought to light: hence the police found it genuinely helpful, but ultimately corroborative rather than crucial.

Disappointed, the police returned to their crime scene routine, but public response to the affair was stirring. A story went around that the woman was made pregnant by a GI, murdered by him and her body taken to the woods for disposal. A similar xenophobia identified her as a gypsy – there was a report of a murder among gypsies camping near the tree. But the police did not think Bella's dress in keeping with the gypsies who, as a social group, tended to bypass the law, keeping their feuds and squabbles to themselves.

Meanwhile the press started to froth and speculate about the 'Tree Murder Riddle'. By Christmas 1943, graffiti started appearing, first in Upper Dean Street, Birmingham, "Who put Bella down the Wych Elm – Hagley Wood". Seemingly the dead woman had been christened. The name and slogan slipped into the popular consciousness like a morbid advertising jingle. The phrase was taken up nearer the scene of the crime. "Who put Luebella down the Wych Elm?" asked one, in nearby Old Hill, followed by, "Hagley Wood Bella", and the most repeated of all, "Who put Bella in the Wych Elm?" The latter regularly appeared on flat surfaces and monuments.

Sometimes it was set down with care and attention as if the scribe was attending to his calling with pride; on other occasions scrawled wildly and carelessly. The police were curious, analysing the chalk and establishing it was the type used in local pubs and schools – on dartboards and blackboards. The words began to appear outside their original geographical context and, inevitably, were attributed to a joker or prankster rather than someone with knowledge proper.

Both childlike and catchy, the phrase more than 'caught on' – it became akin to common parlance. Like the whisper in the undergrowth disclosing the ass's ears of King Midas, it laid claim to a deeper resonance. Murder will out, so Shakespeare said. Who put Bella in the Wych Elm? It was akin to an unsolved, teasing riddle – answer that one if you can. There was an element of anarchy about it that appeared to hint at defective institutions and the larger failures of systems and governments. It was like the living human breath of protest sailing forth on its own, always bobbing up somewhere, cheeky and probing, leaving a little chuckle of mockery in its wake. Acquiring a balladic intensity, bit by bit it engraved itself in the collective memory and merged into the deeper rhetoric of folklore, topography and oral tradition.

For a young woman who had died miserably, anonymously, possessing no voice, no known name or point of origin, it was equivalent to a forlorn, rearguard action on her behalf, finally achieving an eerie immortality that she would never have wished for or remotely imagined. She had been allocated a permanent anchorage in a grim and lonely spot, a gnarled old tree stump in a witches' wood, far away from whatever home she may have cherished, with all the questions attached to her life strangled and choked, yet gaining force by tension of constriction – rearing, shaping themselves and asking who were her father, her mother, what happened to her child, her lover, all these humanly precious, withheld contexts, crying out yet ever denied a healing completion or mark of closure. Who Put Bella in the Wych Elm – who today can walk past Hagley Wood without this childish, mindless, never-to-be-stilled refrain – this pennant of tragedy – flagging itself up and fluttering light on the air?

And, of course, the name Bella holds the charge of witchcraft, belladonna being deadly nightshade, a constituent in nefarious brews and potions. Amid this flurry of unease and rumour, Margaret Murray of University College, London, stepped forward as a witchcraft specialist, saying the severed hand was a sign of a black magic execution. "The very act of placing a body in the hollow of a tree," she pointed out, "is associated with witchcraft. The cult of tree-worship is an ancient one and it is linked with sacrifices. The skeleton alone was left, so one cannot be sure whether the body was marked in any way. The Wych Elm is also significant in terms of witchcraft lore. Whoever committed the murder must have known about the hollow in the tree. The other curious fact about this case is that there were many other hollows where the body could have been more easily hidden. As for the chalk writing on walls in Midland towns, these may have been simply the work of a hoaxer or hoaxers. But Lubella, one of the names used, is a witch's name and for that matter so is Bella. Coincidence perhaps, but strange all the same."

Margaret Murray might have added the Norse God, Odin, was hung on a tree for nine whole nights and stabbed with a spear: hence his title 'God of the Hanged' or 'Lord of the Gallows'. The God of Vegetation was also a tree spirit and the chief god of the Nile, Osiris, took on an arboreal role, with his body being placed in a tree. Frazer refers to a ceremony involving a pine tree being cut down and the centre being hollowed out – an image of Osiris is made from the wood that is buried "like a corpse" in the middle of the tree. This image was taken out and burned after a year.

Unconsciously a man or woman may echo an ancient myth or ritual by an act of unconsidered, random brutality. Although the tree-lore of the ages is a fascinating subject, it cannot be credibly placed on what was, in all probability, a squalid, vicious deed, but such is the macabre oddity of Bella's ending, it is possible for anyone with a

82

knowledge of symbolism or literature, however scrappy, to drape over the desecration a high-sounding precedent or deeper occult purpose that neither mitigates the horror nor facilitates a deeper understanding.

THE DUTCHMAN AND THE TRAPEZE ARTIST

In 1953, Wilfred Byford–Jones, a columnist on the *Wolverhampton Express & Star*, offered a hundred pounds for a solution to the Bella mystery. A plausible account was supplied by a woman called 'Anna' who contacted him, claiming Bella had been murdered for knowing too much about a pro–German spy ring that included a Dutchman, a foreign trapeze artist and a British officer. The Dutchman and trapeze artist killed Bella after she became involved in their circle and acquired information that would endanger them. Apparently Bella was a Dutchwoman who had arrived in England illegally in 1941 and got involved in espionage. Apparently, after deciding she could no longer be trusted, she was killed by the Dutchman and the trapeze artist in a car while driving through Halesowen and then her body was taken to nearby Hagley Wood.

Further meetings and deeper questioning from Byford–Jones loosened Anna's tongue. Her potential for either candour or invention may be judged from the more plausible variant of the same story that she offered, demoting the officer to the lower rank of her husband, Jack Mossop, who merely dressed up like an RAF officer on occasions.

However, Jack *did* work in a munitions factory and befriend a Dutchman called Van Ralt, and Anna, whose real name was Una, suspected Van Ralt was paying Jack for information on the factory. Jack was unstable and their marriage shortly ended. But late in 1941, he looked up Una and confessed to suffering from nightmares. He then described how he met Van Ralt at the Lyttleton Arms in Hagley. The latter was with a Dutchwoman with whom he was arguing. He ordered Jack to drive them to the Clent Hills. Jack took the car out, with Van Ralt and the Dutchwoman in the back, but their dispute became violent and Van Ralt murdered her. Then Jack drove into a layby beside Hagley Wood and helped Van Ralt carry the body into the woods and stuff it inside a hollow tree. That was the last he saw of Van Ralt.

Jack Mossop did not long survive the experience. He was not a well man, mentally or physically, dying in a mental hospital in 1942.

But a report of the time *did* back Una's account, describing a car parked near Hagley Wood area with a man in military uniform in the front seat and a woman apparently sleeping under a coat at the back. But that hardly stands as conclusive and, as Una's story began with a farrago of invention, this more credible variant may have been concocted to secure the £100 payment from Byford-Jones. Was mentally troubled Jack Mossop really privy to important espionage secrets? To merely know the *position* of a munitions factor is all the Luftwaffe needed to bomb it, so why should Jack claim that much attention from Van Ralt? Is this an example of a louche wartime friendship generating an excess of rumour? Was Jack Mossop deluding himself when he related details of the murder?

ENTER CLARABELLA DRONKERS

If Bella was a German spy sent to Hagley in 1940, it was because Goering or his advisors judged it ideal for learning about British aircraft. Lying between the Rolls Royce factory and the airfields at Hartlebury, it was a strategic location from which to make contact with Nazi sympathisers who had earlier infiltrated the region. The latter may have initially assisted Bella and then killed her when they thought their cover might be blown. This theory (allegedly) has the support of papers uncovered in Germany which refer to a woman of Bella's appearance whose dental records are 'almost' a match.

In the chapters on Bella in *Murder by Witchcraft*, Donald McCormick pursued the espionage angle with zeal, setting it against the background of planted and parachuted Nazi agents from Holland entering Britain in 1941 and attempting to undermine the British intelligence network and, of course, the counter-measures taken against them by the MI5, possibly involving murder. He describes contacting an ex-Nazi called Herr Franz Rathgeb, who had spent time in the English Midlands during the war, and knew a German agent named Lehrer. The latter had a girlfriend who was also a German spy, a Dutchwoman possibly called 'Clarabella Dronkers', who had lived in Birmingham, was about 30, and had irregular teeth.

It is known that a Dutchman named Johannes Marinus Dronkers was executed for spying by the British in December 1942, but whether there was ever a Clarabella Dronkers has never been proven. But McCormick, diligent super-sleuth, discovers through Rathgeb a Frau

Cremer in Amsterdam who might be able to assist. McCormick contacts this lady and receives a helpful letter in which she states that she knew Frau Dronkers who "posed as a friend of the Dutch Resistance" but regularly made mysterious trips to Germany, hinting at a more sinister allegiance. Although not a witch, Frau Dronkers was seriously interested in astrology and occultism and was superstitious about the number thirteen. Among her more intimate effects was "a garter of green snakeskin, which was sufficiently unusual to draw comment, especially as a garter of this kind is said to be a witch's band."

A garter of green snakeskin – indeed. One has to salute McCormick for dredging up this fragment of antique naughtiness, but was it derived from Frau Cremer who, in all probability, did not exist anymore than did Frau Dronkers? McCormick is expert at passing the parcel in order to lay a false trail. He eases the reader in by means of known historical names and details and then, adding a falsehood or two, gradually works up to a climax. A fuller examination of his method of assembling an ostensibly factual work is provided in the chapter *Murder by Witchcraft*.

False trails aside, there *is* evidence of Nazi activity and attempts to infiltrate the Midland area. Two German parachutists were said to have landed and vanished in the Hagley area, early in 1941. This bulked out the Bella 'spy' theory, but did not quite deliver. Say, if Bella were a Nazi agent, British Intelligence would have arrested and interrogated her. If she were an Anti-Nazi spy, who had penetrated the Abwehr network, contact with the MI5 might have been expected.

If her true identity had been rumbled by the Nazi conclave she was penetrating, it is implausible they would have subjected her to a woodland assault, choked her and cut off her hand. The mutilation might be regarded as a ploy, but there is little point in weaving a plot worthy of Baroness Orczy around a tragedy so mute and unyielding.

Attempts to enmesh Bella in a spying conspiracy may seem farfetched – if one considers how few women back then in Britain were foreign spies and the statistical likelihood of any coming to an end like that. Perhaps there has been too much dwelling on spying, mythology and witchcraft, bypassing the commonplace observation that brutal assaults were not that uncommon in wartime. There were good soldiers and bad soldiers. In fact, a trooper of the Great War confessed to a mate that the army provided him the only opportunity he ever had to behave

85

totally like an animal – visit the most degrading and awful punishments upon the human body without danger of arrest. To list the many bloody assaults upon women during this period would be futile, but suffice to add that the local parasearcher, David Taylor, after a television appearance, was contacted by an old lady in the area who told him that, as a young girl going to work on the bus in the 1940's, "she remembers going past Hagley Wood and seeing a 'gypsy' girl covered in blood being chased by a man with a stick or club, but she decided to say nothing because it was the war! A woman, covered in blood, in the right place at the right time! Unfortunately the description doesn't match the remains found!"

BELLA'S SHOES

As with Charles Walton, because of the paucity of living witnesses, the few bits of clothing and personal effects of Bella were utilised to play a highly significant role in detection, especially her shoes. The latter attracted expert testimony and analysis when a gentleman called Mr Cogzell, a former shoemaker, identified the markings on Bella's crêpe soles saying that he could shed light on the crime by tracing the style of stitching to a local cobbler. So a request was put in at Birmingham University Medical School for Dr Griffiths, Professor Webster's replacement, to make available the shoes. But Dr Griffiths responded in an irate manner, saying there was no skeleton and no shoes. The former had definitely gone missing.

When Mr Cogzell persisted, the doctor picked up a pair of shoes and threw them at him[5] – but they were not Bella's crêpe soles apparently. Naturally from this incident arose cries of a cover-up. Was the loss of Bella's body a desperate ploy? Professor Webster had loaned it to a colleague who had no idea where he placed it. This gave rise to a rumour the body *had* been identified and the authorities, for their own reasons, wanted enquiries to cease. Was their disinclination to make a clean breast of the affair connected with vital, incriminatory information or mere incompetence, similar to a present-day minister who mislays his briefcase or computer holding vital information? No arrests or detailed apologies followed.

---

[5] This thrilling response was denied by an official source who pointed out that Dr Griffiths was a courteous gentleman – in no way a shoe-hurling type.

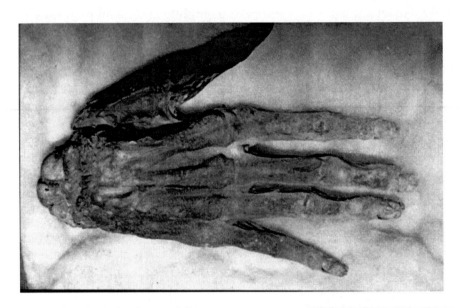

Above: Hand of Glory, gruesome lucky charm.
Below: Bella graffiti on the obelisk on Wychbury Hill.

MURDER BY WITCHCRAFT

B efore starting this book, I studied authors who had previously treated the subject. Articles were available on 'Bella' and the Walton Murder, mostly useful summaries, but only one thorough, book-length study, *Murder by Witchcraft* (1964) by Donald McCormick, a popular writer of non-fiction who had worked with Ian Fleming in Naval Intelligence and brought out a history of the British Secret Service and other espionage titles under the pseudonym Richard Deacon.

Murder by Witchcraft is an easy, enjoyable read by a fluent and versatile author, a splendid amassment of information collating news articles of the time, forensic detail, legend and lore aplenty, combined with interviews and anecdotes from the locals of Lower Quinton as well as distinguished scholars like Margaret Murray.

It was written at the outset of that occult wave that later swept through British society as the Church of England lost its hold and people started to pursue strange gods and question old certainties. It is only lightly relevant as a police investigation – for the important primary sources were not available for perusal. What narrative there is becomes subsumed in the bulk of topography, occultism and espionage pervading the text. There is even a confession of helplessness appealingly buried there:

I seemed to be going round in circles. The problem when an author tries to be an amateur detective is that he is apt to become too interested in playing with ideas and in the purely literary aspect of what he discovers. Shrewd as he may flatter himself to be, the subconscious mind will too often draw from facts to fantasy. There really was no reason why I should have pursued this line of enquiry other than the fact I was sucked into it like a bobbing cork. Yet there is some excuse: the two Midland murders had baffled all detectives who had investigated them, so a certain amount of off-beat research might yet pay off.

This is honest – for some passages convey the impression the book's subject is Cotswold and Warwickshire witch legends.

Other chapters plunge into the glamorous world of the spy –
another of McCormick's specialisations – with fertile speculation on
Nazi agents in the Midlands, Goebbels's campaign of astrological
propaganda and Herr Hess's fixation on the occult that prompted MI5
to knock on Aleister Crowley's door.

The author gives his impression of arriving at Lower Quinton in
a captivating way:

I deliberately visited Lower Quinton for the first time in midsummer because
I wanted to avoid being over-influenced by the bleakness of a Cotswold
winter. That, I could well imagine, would induce a feeling that one was
wandering along dark lanes while the winds wailed in banshee fashion as one
approached the House of Usher. But for the subtle, visual quality of eeriness I
was not prepared. Perhaps, it might be argued, I was subconsciously imposing
on what I saw.

To discover the hidden secret of the village, enter the church that
displays symbolism harking back to a more ruthless age:

The scene was peaceful enough in the sunlight of June: thatched and timbered
cottages around a village green and a beautiful little church with seven styles
of architecture, Saxon, Norman, thirteenth century and other periods. But a
closer examination of the church gave one an even deeper visual impression
of the macabre. For over the chancel arch was carved a sixteenth-century
coat-of-arms, comprising a unicorn raging at a winged dragon with ferocious
jaws and hideous claws, all red and yellow and black, and underneath in bold,
black letters: God love our noble Queen Elizabeth, Amen!

With its 127-foot spire and spacious arcades, St Swithin's is a radiant,
imposing parish church, but the coat-of-arms does not look *that* scary
in the well-lit interior. However, McCormick does supply some of the
chatter and rumour extant in the 1960s. I was engaged by much of what
I read, noticing that significant revelations were provided by an
'anonymous' farmer or 'a local of my acquaintance' or an enigmatic
'High Priestess' – all providing, I hasten to add, lively comments, but
how true were they? Protecting people by not naming them may be a
courtesy but it may also provide a cover for false information.

EXPOSÉ

Knowing of journalists, their manner of pointing and exaggerating, so that the scenario might appear more dramatically in keeping, especially in 'suspect' areas like witchcraft and diabolical hooey, I began to doubt McCormick's access to telling facts that evaded lesser men, particularly in the allegedly mute, tight-lipped village of Lower Quinton and its environs. Was it his charm or innate ability to look in the right places – or something else? Mildly suspicious, I took a closer look at McCormick's literary profile to find out what others thought. I was not surprised to learn that he was considered 'creative' in his deployment of source material – inclined to quote extensively from people who may or may not exist. But I was surprised by Melvin Harris's truly devastating online deconstruction of his reputation.

In a detailed, entertaining exposé, Melvin Harris pointed out that Donald McCormick had two books published in 1959: *The Identity of Jack the Ripper* and *The Mystery of Lord Kitchener's Death*. The second of these initially interested Harris. He was working for BBC Radio and contacted McCormick after Radio Four had broadcast a drama based on the Kitchener book. He had become preoccupied with a 1926 hoax by the journalist Frank Power, thinking it might make a radio programme. Power located an "undivulged mystery in the story of Kitchener's death" that the Admiralty was hiding. Going into this, Melvin was struck by how botched was McCormick's version:

When I started to research the Frank Power story I found that McCormick's account was badly flawed. He told us that the hoaxer Power had been the *The Times's* correspondent at the siege of Khartoum (1884) and had written the historic 'Letters from Khartoum'. This was absurd. *The Times's* reporter and British Consul at Khartoum in 1884 was the famous war correspondent Frank Le Poer Power, who was killed in September 1884!

Later, in 1981, Melvin started looking into hoaxers on the subject of Jack the Ripper – foremost slasher of them all – reading McCormick's 1959 study *The Identity of Jack the Ripper*. This quakingly dark subject would seem a useful apprenticeship for the later project of the Lower Quinton murder.

So how did McCormick square up as a Ripper-Investigator? Harris was not impressed by either the first work or the expanded version that followed. Reading them inspired him to set up a TV programme for Ripperologists – a Court Room 'question and answer session' following an inquest pattern ('How Unimpeachable are Your Sources?' instead of 'How Clean is Your Home?'). For the pillory he singled out the "leading living fakers", namely Joseph Sickert, Frank Spiering and Donald McCormick. Allowing his estimates of the trio were correct, one might imagine they'd prefer to decline the honour of being subjected to a documentary dressing-down in public and then asked to confess their culpability, after which Melvin would dismiss them with some sort of popelike gesture of absolution for having so abased themselves.

What was plain was *The Identity of Jack the Ripper* (1959) contained a quantity of 'new' – if convoluted – Russian material that came by way of William Le Queux, Gregori Rasputin and the jottings of Dr Dutton, an associate of Inspector Frederick Abberline, who had a close knowledge of Whitechapel and supervised the investigation. Names and diary entries are shuffled so masterfully that the reader bows to anyone who can make top or tail of such dextrous scrabblings and, just to make matters perfectly obscure, a Jack the Ripper 'double' called Pedachenko – a obstetrician from Tver who was in London at the time of the murders – is nailed as the arch criminal.

Aside from incriminating foreigners, McCormick supplied an anonymous verse, allegedly sent to the police in Autumn of 1888:

Eight little whores, with no hope of heaven,
Gladstone may save one, then there'll be seven.
Seven little whores begging for a shilling,
One stays in Henage Court, then there's a killing.
Six little whores, glad to be alive,
One sidles up to Jack, then there are five.
Four and whore rhyme aright,
So do three and me,
I'll set the town alight
Ere there are two.
Two little whores, shivering with fright,
Seek a cosy doorway in the middle of the night.

Jack's knife flashes, then there's but one,
And the last one's the ripest for Jack's idea of fun.

The idea of Melvin's TV programme was dropped, but dubious studies of the Ripper continued to appear. Because of the quantity of hearsay and invention that had insinuated itself into what purported to be a historical discipline, Melvin decided that the heterogeneous mass of Ripper Studies should be reassessed and the valid separated from the dross. Instead of accepting the provenance of any old letter, diary or poem allegedly recovered from a bloodstained suitcase or car boot sale in the district of Whitechapel, a scholarly rigour was to be applied. Too many writers had been drawing on dubious or faked material in order to starch up their arguments. In fact, bogus sources had been quoted so often and duplicated in so many works that someone new to the game might be totally led astray. Unless some sort of agreement as to what constituted a valid source could be reached, the whole corpus would end up tainted and debased.

With this in mind, Melvin decided to contact McCormick and inform him of his intention. He had heard that his health was not good and did not want to launch a full-scale offensive for which the older man would be unprepared. So he rang him and explained the nature of his crusade, adding that he had looked into his book on the Ripper and found it suspect. Deeper into the discussion, he bluntly suggested "none of the material alleged to be from Dr Dutton was accurate or even historically acceptable." He enumerated the lies and misstatements so concisely that McCormick, knowing the game was up, conceded he had nowhere to hide:

He became philosophical about his exposure, especially when I said that I was prepared to describe the fakery as the work of a man with a wicked sense of humour. I stated that I was not going to ask for the name of the faker unless he wished to divulge it. Specifically, though, I drew his attention to the poem about the 'Eight little whores'. I was struck by the way that writers had cheerfully quoted these lines without any misgivings, and used them as if they were authentic verses from 1888. At that time they had been used by Odell, Farson, Prof. Camps, Rumbelow, Cullen and Michael Harrison.

Melvin Harris put it to McCormick that the 'Eight Little Whores' verses had no antiquity, being unknown before appearing in his book in 1959. The other hesitated and tried to blarney round the point. Not wanting to appear antagonistic, Melvin abandoned stark confrontation and devised an escape route for his quarry. He offered to refer to the verses as the work of a "very clever man who enjoys his quiet fun." McCormick accepted that compassionate, slightly flattering estimate and admitted the story was made up, taking its impetus from a 1930s forgery.

Although Melvin had made dramatic progress, the word was not yet out, and he needed McCormick to explain or admit more. What proportion of material had he uncovered as opposed to forging?

So I wrote to him in 1990 and queried his use. Then in a following letter I wrote this: My question about the 'Eight little whores...' verse was not meant to be a catch question, but simply to find out where you took it from.

Melvin was forcing McCormick into a corner. He knew that, far from being a discovery, the verse was a composition, the author of whom took pride in misleading and taking the reader on a merry dance. "It was, in fact, concocted by McCormick," Melvin concluded. "His book is a deliberate fraud. Everything, his quotes from Dutton, from Belloselski, from Backert, from 'the London doctor who knew Sickert and whose father was at Oxford with Druitt', has been invented by him."

Eventually Harris met up with McCormick in the flesh. By this time the 'Jack the Ripper Diary' had been published – another hoax drawing material from McCormick's earlier forgeries. By now, Harris thought it was really time for a day of reckoning. At the book signing at Camille Wolff's, Harris and McCormick talked. The former pointed out the 'Diary' hoax had agitated the problem yet again, adding another irritating layer of deception, and he wanted "to set the record straight in a new book" that would filter out the rubbish and clarify things.

Harris then asked McCormick to name the man or woman who had faked the notorious Jack the Ripper jingle, but the latter declined, adding he preferred to retain the guise of "a very clever man who enjoys his quiet fun", and winked at his inquisitor as though trying to entice him into the conspiracy.

Melvin commented:

Yes, he was a likeable rogue. But he was trapped by his very likeability. Over the years he had kept up the bluff with so many people that he found it hard to disentangle himself, as I found out when I later wrote to him. He was, by then, unwilling to commit himself in writing, instead he wrote letters full of teasing, enigmatic clues.

In October 1997, Harris wrote yet again and asked him to set the record straight and submit an honest account of his 'discoveries' or inventions. The reply came back that McCormick was ill – he had an ulcer on his right eye and was unable to write: 'Please let the matter drop.'

From the standpoint of probity, Harris was right to demand the truth, but McCormick feared the sort of outright admission he was after would not only ruin his reputation in the world of writing, but leave him open to being sued or at best disowned by his own publishers for touting fraudulent research. McCormick died soon after without making a final confession.

While not inspiring confidence, Harris's exposure did not lead to me to dismiss *Murder by Witchcraft* as worthless. Some of the sources cited remain relevant and verifiable, and often the summaries of known events are adequate. As for the occult material drawn from recycled newspaper stories, that *was* spurious, being in the main cobbled from the gossip of would-be witches. Usually the latter were bribed to devise a spicy-to-moderately-shocking feature, inevitably deficient in verifiable detail. For instance, imagine browsing the headline 'Witches Sacrifice Virgin at Party'. If lacking names, addresses or notice of police intervention, who is likely to be convinced? Yet it gains a spurious authority by appearing as 'news' – any old lie so long as it's in print. Scraping the demonic greasepaint off such reporting hardly merits the effort.

WITCHING UP OLD CHARLIE

Yet, to be fair, McCormick's prose is a few rungs above the average diabolic waffle. The area in which I had to be circumspect was in treating as 'evidence' his unnamed landowners, alleged contacts of Charles Walton or middle-class high priestesses of occult orders who spontaneously materialise to diversify his material. Even in the instance of the latter, they usually echo allegations or propositions already in the air. Their most notable distortion was in making a warlock out of Old Charlie and, in the case of Bella, spectacularly amplifying the espionage angle.

It is far from clear what McCormick has extrapolated and invented as opposed to honestly recorded. There are many lively asides and anecdotes that it would be unfair to totally dismiss – after all, presumably he *did* visit Lower Quinton and speak to locals who were present at the time of the murder – but parts read as a wee bit 'actorish', the type of dialogue a scriptwriter might produce for a tale of local intrigue.

Here he is ventriloquising for an inhabitant of Long Compton:

"Old Charlie was a bit odd, but he kept his oddities to himself. In everyday life he was as normal as you or I and he was never in any cult. Of that I am sure. He had a wealth of country lore, he knew all the gossip about witches and he was in his early days fascinated by the subject, but as he grew older he never talked about it. Occasionally, when he had a few ciders, he would say knowingly that he had seen witches' rites performed at the Rollright Stones and he insisted that such thing still went on. He was cunning in his way and a bit of a Peeping Tom – not in the usual way, but as a youth he had spied on the covens. Or so he said. He knew what they did and where they met."

Had he attempted to appease the witches? What about the black glass he carried with him?

"He reckoned it brought him luck. He once said to me, 'If it doesn't bring me good luck, it keeps off the bad luck. If ever I'm working for anyone I don't trust, I keep that glass with me."

What, I asked, did he mean.

"With Old Charlie you could never really tell. It might have meant anything or nothing. He didn't have any obvious enemies, no one you could name. But he had an uncanny instinct... He knew instinctively if anyone disliked him, or wanted to trick him. I remember once when I was with him inwardly laughing at him and then having a tremendous feeling of guilt, because I sensed Charles knew exactly what I was thinking."

Penetrating McCormick's fabrications may not involve hard work or prolonged research because quite often he does it for you. He will produce a story or anecdote that is mildly astounding and then, quite honestly, add that he doubts the truth of it, later slipping in the point he wants most to impress on the reader. So, although he has denied the credibility of the allegation, he has flourished it sufficiently to prepare your mind for what he wants to say which may well turn out to be a further bluff.

An aspect of Old Charlie that McCormick highlights was his ability to engage with animals and nature. Quite literally, Walton would 'speak to the birds' who fed out of his hand. He was able to direct them where to alight – furthermore he claimed to translate "every chirrup and tweet" of their language. The latter is 'charming' and not to be dismissed as purely McCormick's fantasising. There are many alive today who claim these skills, but was Walton one of them? If only Walton's niece Edie had claimed that for him or his best friend George Higgins, one might have felt on safer ground.

McCormick also contacted a High Priestess of a Warwickshire coven who confided her opinions of Charles Walton's occult status:

"As you can see for yourself, there is no evidence whatsoever of sacrificial killings in modern witchcraft…But fear of witchcraft is hard to remove, harder in some country areas, especially in Warwickshire…As soon as witchcraft is mentioned as a possible motive in the Lower Quinton murder case, people immediately assume it was ordained by some coven. It was even suggested that Charles Walton was the member of a coven and that he was sentenced to death for revealing its secrets. That is nonsense, too. I assure you the modern practitioners of witchcraft, inside or outside of covens, are not to be found among hedgers and farm labourers. They come mainly from the professional classes and this would have been just as true during the war as today. All I know of witchcraft in this area during the war, when it was very spasmodically practised, was that it was partly a form of escape from the rigours of war and, more often, used as an invocation for victory. We used the unity of the witches to express through our religion – and it is a religion – our will to defeat the Germans. Some covens used the same technique when the flying bombs came over in the last year of the war. It is of course wicked to accuse this poor old man of being mixed up in some kind of black magic, or to suggest he was malevolently disposed to his neighbours. He was not a member of the cult, though he may have certainly known something about it. What Old Charlie possessed was a strange kind of psychic power which you get in some countrymen. Sometimes it shows in their instinct for amazingly accurate weather forecasting, or for dowsing and divining with hazel twigs. More often – and this *was* true of Charles – it is revealed in an uncanny understanding of animals and birds and being able to communicate with them."

The High Priestess goes on to say Old Charlie was far more like the old-fashioned idea of a witch or warlock than the witches and warlocks of today: "Nobody would expect a man with a rolled umbrella and a bowler hat to be a warlock, yet that is really what he well might be. But find a harmless old gipsy woman whose face is wrinkled and pock-marked and people with say she is a witch."

In her view, the killer misinterpreted Charlie as a man of occult power, "capable of bringing disaster to crops, livestock and the killer himself": hence this hot-tempered countryman, reverting to the tradition of his ancestors, 'stanged' Old Charlie good and proper.

McCormick also spoke to 'Mr Blank', a retired farmer who lived at Long Compton and had known Charles Walton well, employing him on several occasions. He did not want his name to be mentioned but claimed Charles Walton was obsessed with toads and used to play with them for hours:

"He believed toads were lucky. He wouldn't kill them. Now the toads we get in England are not large, not more than three and a half inches as a rule and the female ones are the largest. Now if you get a natterjack toad, the legs are so short they can't hop, but they can run quite fast. Old Charlie used to catch a toad and tie a toy plough to its leg and have it run along towing the thing across a field. Now there's not anything frightening in that to the ordinary person, is there? But he used to say to me, *When I pull that trick on, he gets real scared and mad at me…*"

Aside from the toad's understandable disinclination to be harnessed, this is a direct snatch from the Scottish witch, Isobel Gowdie, who was tried and put to death in 1692 for making crops barren and cattle sicken by conniving a toad to draw a toy plough across a field. Naturally McCormick invokes Isobel as a precedent; already familiar with her confession, he foisted her stratagem on Charlie, bridging past and present and creating a symmetry pleasing to readers.

The advantage McCormick enjoyed was that Charlie's living 'friends' were probably toothless and far from highly literate communicators. They would not be the types to challenge or correct the authority of a glib, seasoned journalist and writer of popular non-fiction. Hence, as with his book on Jack the Ripper, McCormick's 'factions' went largely unchallenged and it became more or less established that Charles was a witch or 'cunning man' who spoke to birds and toads.

The latter attribute was taken up by Cecil Williamson who seldom acknowledges the texts from which he lifts information, pretending it all came from the horse's mouth.

There's an eagerness on the part of some to frame Walton as a witch who was killed by another witch or witches in a premeditated murder. This provocative thesis flowed into the bloodstream of the reportage and drastically re-shaped the career of a quiet-living countryman. For instance, Simon Read's online article, *In Cold Blog*, presents Old Charlie as a teenager developing his supernatural abilities:

His powers of clairvoyance supposedly came to him in his younger years when he worked the fields of nearby Meon Hill, a bleak place that was once believed to be the earthly dwelling of Satan. On three consecutive evenings while walking home after long days harvesting the fields, Walton claimed to have seen a phantom black dog sitting on the slope of the hill and watching him in the fading light of day. On the third night, a headless woman accompanied the dog. The two spectres stood motionless, side by side, as the evening ground mist swirled about them.

The following day, Walton's sister died.

The young man, overcome with grief, believed the ghostly hound and its headless owner had come to him as omens. The strange episode instilled an everlasting fear of dogs and all but nullified his ability to socialize with others. He became an introvert who took odd jobs for poor pay and shunned the company of others. Because of the change in his behaviour, the village folk began to suspect that Walton had taken up with a coven of witches and was taking part in strange nocturnal rituals on the outskirts of Lower Quinton. Walton never denied such speculation, and his reputation for the bizarre only grew.

Taken as a portrait drawing upon the available sources, Simon Read has produced an entertaining summary of the case, eloquent and exciting, but his quick-developing young psychic has little in common with the prosaic, steady-going old labourer who was uncle to Edie.

Another facet of Walton's character, rather slyly trumpeted by McCormick, was his propensity to load a wheelbarrow with large quantities of cider which he took back to his house and drank by himself. These liquid extravaganzas were never recorded by his niece, Edie, who said of her uncle: "He was an extremely good-tempered man. I have never known him to lose his temper or use bad language. I have never heard him speak or have a quarrel with anyone.
He was friendly with everyone but no one ever visited him at the house. He didn't go out in the evenings and seldom went to a public house."

In support of this, Professor Webster, who performed the autopsy, emphasised Walton was "a remarkably healthy old man", most of his internal organs in excellent condition for a man of his years, and his liver was "a normal-sized organ" showing "no evidence of cirrhosis or back pressure" and his gall bladder and bladder were in fine condition too. Only his skeletal system indicated change owing to age and osteo-arthritis.

DECONSTRUCTING THE SUPERNATURAL

In the superficial accounts he wrote for popular consumption, Inspector Fabian drew attention to the similarities in the way Charles Walton and Ann Tennant were killed. A pitchfork *was* used in both instances, but Ann was stabbed repeatedly with the implement in broad daylight while spectators looked on aghast. No billhook was used to cross-slash her body as in the Lower Quinton killing. James Hayward was tried, declared mad and placed in Broadmoor Criminal Lunatic Asylum. There he died at the age of 59 in 1890.

What of the Charles Walton in the Reverend Bloom's book?

The latter young man, who was haunted by the apparition of the Black Dog, came from Alveston while Old Charlie had his roots in Lower Quinton. The confusion was clarified by shrewd genealogical research carried out by 'Police Inspector Appleby' who posted it online *(Jack the Ripper: Casebook Forums)*. Charles Walton, he pointed out, had three older sisters and two younger brothers.

Between May and June in 1885 and the same months in 1886, he would have been 15 years old. According to Bloom, this was his age when he met the spectral dog previous to the death of his sister. If the Charles Walton in the story was the same 'Old Charlie' who was murdered in 1945 in Lower Quinton, he would need to have had a sister who died a year or less after the black dog encounter. Old Charlie's sisters were called Mary Ann Walton and Martha Walton. As both married in 1891 and lived on for some years, they were obviously not affected. His third sister Harriett – actually his step-sister – was still alive in 1901.

This led Appleby to conclude Bloom's anecdote portrayed another Charles Walton "unless Emma, his mother, gave birth to a fourth daughter between the April 1881 Census and the early summer of 1886."

"The 1841 Census, taken on 7 June 1841, conveniently records Charles's mother as being just 9 months old, implying that she was born around August or September 1840. In April 1881 she would have been almost 41 years old, without having given birth – at least to a living child – for some five or six years. I believe it is highly unlikely that she did so during the next five years, especially since a detailed study of the birth, marriage and death records held by the Office of National Statistics has failed to produce any likely children's births or deaths being registered in the Shipston or Stratford-upon-Avon areas during that period."

'Inspector Appleby' has performed a spirited deconstruction of that little myth. However, to be fair, Bloom's work is a relaxed, anecdotal book, mingling fact, gossip and folklore. Such topographical musings are seldom written by zealots of exactitude. In fact, many brim with inaccuracies simply because they would take five times as long to write if everything was date-checked and correlated. So, allowing for a little latitude, the Reverend Bloom may not have done *that* bad a job and, quite possibly, young Charlie Walton did work at Alveston for a period. Bloom could have been writing about the same man but transcribed the facts wrongly. Whether Walton did or did not see the Black Dog, or whether his sister lived or died within the specified period, are matters that enrich the supernatural dimension.

THE REMARKABLE VISION OF MR ELWELL

Murder strikes most people – especially parents or spouses of victims – as an outrage, a blight on mankind. If the murderer stays undetected, anxiety and unease may intensify. Those closest to the casualty imagine their loved one hovering in a spiritual limbo, awaiting the justice that life has held back. An alliance forms between the world of the living and that of the dead. Some enforce contact by dreaming – a traditional way of crossing over. Whenever hunters of the chamois fell to their deaths on the Alpine peaks where they pursued their lonely calling, it was said that, on the night of the tragedy, their wives would dream of the particular crevasse, cliff-edge or chasm into which their spouses had fallen. Hence, when day dawned, the search party would know from where to recover the frozen corpse. Associated with this area of psychic expertise are 'crisis apparitions' that appear warning relatives of an impending or simultaneously occurring disaster. They are like urgent signals from fatality's frontier – attempts to alert the living of oncoming peril and bereavement

In 1922 a rather rakish young man named Eric Tombe went missing. He had been in partnership with a reckless, spendthrift called Dyer who had been launching big schemes in horse-racing and motoring, spending lavishly on girl friends and using up Tombe's money in a high-handed, reckless way. When Tombe literally vanished, his parents were both anxious and suspicious and his clergyman father turned detective and began to seek out his missing boy. He knew he had been involved with Dyer who had by then accidentally shot himself while pursuing criminal activities under the name of James Fitzsimmons. The clergyman's researches awakened the interest of the great British detective of the day, Francis Carlin, who was convinced Dyer had been responsible for Tombe's absence. Yet he could find no evidence of a missing body on The Welcomes, the farmhouse, race-horse training and stud stables Dyer had obtained through Tombe's money. Then the clergyman told Carlin that his wife was having this shocking dream, night after night, in which she saw her son's body lying at the foot of a well. Carlin was sympathetic but dubious.

101

A day or two later, he and his team were down at The Welcomes when he discovered something that shocked him – there were disused wells[6] in the grounds of the house. Instantly he gave his men the order: "Dig." They set to work, digging twelve feet down, until they exposed a human foot sticking out of black, oily mud. Hence the body of poor young Tombe was recovered.

In a similar manner, people dreamed strange dreams, saw apparitions and had intimations about the murders of Charles Walton and Bella. An instance of this occurred in 1955 when a railway clerk, Mr George Elwell, claimed to have solved the Bella case. He was able to name both victim and perpetrator of the crime. Mr Elwell, a citizen of Wollaston, near Stourbridge, came from the area and had been taking regular walks in Hagley Wood. The skeleton of Bella keenly interested him and one night, walking through the wood, he stopped by the tree stump and stood there for ten minutes trying to establish contact with whatever he sensed was there. Back at his home in Wollaston, he decided to conduct an experiment in self-hypnosis by shining a light bulb onto a shaving mirror that he set up before his face. "The bulb," he explained, "shines through a revolving disc, giving a flickering effect, and by this means I was able to lull myself into a trance."

By his side, Mr Elwell had a tape-recorder borrowed from a friend and set running so that it might take down whatever insights occurred during the trance. When he snapped out of it and played back the tape, a melodramatic message came through. "It is very cold," he heard himself say. "There's a horse neighing somewhere...rain drops on the trees...dark, very dark...a tree, yes...what's he got on his shoulder? Oh, God, untying string...Oh, my God...blood on her face! Blood down her face on her hair...Oh, she's dead, she's dead. Now name, what is her name? Bradman, that's it...Annie Bradley of Leeds..."

And he added that her killer had a moustache, was tall and probably a serviceman.

---

[6] Phil Baker's splendid biography of Dennis Wheatley, *The Devil is a Gentleman*, has a detailed account of Tombe who emerges as a louche, self-educated if rather attractive bounder, introducing Wheatley to the literature of the Decadents, the Russian classics and works on philosophy and religion. His dreadfully decomposed body is not described as being found in a well but in about ten feet of filthy dark water, one of the cesspits attached to the farm.

With due seriousness, the police followed up this information, making enquiries in Leeds about missing women, and were unable to learn anything about Annie Bradley.

At a more practical level, local author Joyce Coley interviewed Warwick Plant whose parents owned a public house *The Crown* near Hagley Wood. During the war, Warwick remembered how a small woman called Bella came into the pub, asking his mother whether she might entertain customers by singing and playing the piano. When Mrs Plant agreed, Bella confided that she was a member of a concert party who'd travelled Europe but had come to England with the outbreak of war. On a cold, wet day, Bella arrived, poorly shod, soaked to the skin and shivering. Taking her in hand, Mrs Plant placed her before the fender in the kitchen and gave her a pair of crêpe-soled shoes for which she expressed a touching gratitude. For a time, she entertained at the pub, singing and playing, her favourite number being, 'If I were a Blackbird'. Then, abruptly, she stopped coming to *The Crown* and was never seen again. Could her screams have rent the peace of the wood during the parachute drop of 1941 or did she merely move out of the area?

Bella told Warwick's mother that she had an uneasy relationship with her landlord who would beat her from time to time. This slightly forlorn woman seems more real than the shadowy secret agent of Byford-Jones's regular column. It derives from a single, solid source rather than patchwork details. On the other hand, Mrs Plant makes no mention of Bella's dental abnormality, her irregular teeth, so the identification is far from conclusive.

THE GHOST OF BELLA

After the 1950s, the history of Bella did not develop. The circumstantial facts had been long-established, but the body had gone, leaving no chance of a forensic breakthrough producing fresh evidence. Without likelihood of any new disclosures, the legend could only be nourished by hacks, psychics and artists who found inspiration in the mystery and pathos of the never-identified woman. Especially the composer, Simon Holt, who confided his fascination with the theme after reading Simon Askwith's article in *The Independent*:

"Bella's macabre story has become part of local mythology in South West Birmingham. Everybody has their own angle on who or what she was. When I visited the area at the beginning of 2003, I stopped two octogenarians out for a stroll, who told me that they thought she had probably been "on the game", as they put it. They laughed uneasily when I asked them if they had known her personally. As I left them, to walk up Wychbury Hill towards the obelisk on the Hagley Hall estate, I noticed four teenagers adding their own graffiti to the confusion of cryptic signs and arcane scratchings scrawled around its base. One of them was called Matty (a name I would use for the boy who had been the first to discover 'Bella's body down the tree: he would soon die after from the shock, and bird's-nesting would never be the same again for the other two boys). I asked him if he knew anything about 'Bella', and he instantly became cagey, as if it were too touchy a subject to embark on, particularly with a complete stranger. I was amazed to discover very fresh-looking graffito, in thick white paint, on the western side of the obelisk declaring: "Who put Bella in the Witch elm", almost as if the body has only just been found."

From this powerful curiosity arose Holt's gripping opera *Who Put Bella in the Wych Elm?* Although its première at Aldeburgh drew mixed reviews, the theme's dramatic potency secured a wide press coverage. It portrays Bella as a moody, mercurial barmaid in a local pub who had an 'effect' on her customers before abruptly vanishing. The story employs a flashback format, starting with the old man who discovered the corpse when he was a boy. His troubled ruminations are the handle of the plot – there are hints that he may have been the murderer and desecrator of the corpse.

"Poor Bella," Simon Holt concluded, "whoever and wherever you are – *Rest In Peace*. You have become more vivid to us in death than you possibly ever could have done in life."

The storyline utilised some of the ghostly antics reported at the Gypsy's Tent pub (now the Badgers Sett) near Wychbury Hill and Hagley Wood. David Taylor, head of the UK paranormal research group 'Parasearch', was taken there by his mother as a boy. She worked at the pub in the late 1970s and he heard many stories of the premises being haunted. Doors would open on their own, objects move around and cold spots appear. The staff blamed it on a ghost whom they called 'Bella', owing to the proximity of the murder site. It was also whispered that 'Bella' had been a barmaid in the pub who had met a tragic end.

INSIDE HAGLEY WOOD

I had briefly made email contact with David, who was a friend of local historian, Joyce Coley. She had produced a thorough, gripping study *Bella An Unsolved Murder* that was brought out by HIP (History Into Print). David told me that he and Joyce would be glad to see me when I visited the area and share what they knew. In September, after completing a draft of the book, I went up to stay the night at the Premier Inn beside the Badgers Sett, where David's mother had worked and Bella was alleged to haunt.

I did not tell anyone the purpose of my visit. I did not want to enhance my social profile by confiding I was seeking the location of a murder that took place seventy years ago of a person unknown by a person unknown. If that was not seriously weird, the skeleton of the victim had gone missing too. Even with the assistance of every wandering spirit, oracle and wayside god, there would be difficulty in establishing anything at all. So any seeker needed to be armed with an almost religious faith in his own acuity. I was not. Still, a goal so palpably hopeless is bound to attract pilgrims of a woefully optimistic bent.

I met David and Joyce at the Badgers Sett on Wednesday at 7.15 pm. Clad in a black, gothic style polo neck, he was hale-looking, stocky with black, brushed-back hair and dark eyes that were keen and alert. He had that warm, affable manner I have come to associate with Midlanders. By contrast, Joyce was small, elegant with a shrewd, kindly face and an enquiring glance. Quickly we settled into a discussion that covered Bella, road ghosts, Avebury, witchcraft, coincidences, historical apparitions, the whiles of the publishing world and the problem of distilling truth from supernatural hearsay. Both possessed a far greater local knowledge than me: thus I was able to learn a lot.

For my part, I emphasised no one knew who Bella was. Her very name depended on the trustworthiness of an anonymous graffiti artist who flourished it seemingly from nowhere eight months after her body had been found, around two years after the crime had been committed. The only evidence proper had been the body and that had vanished or been stolen – a nice touch to round off the black farce. David acknowledged the difficulty but still found the eerie pathos

105

fascinating. He admitted leaning towards the spy theory – that Bella was a foreign implant who could not be identified through British records. Therefore the murder had been done for reasons of secrecy. I was doubting but on the other hand had been told by an expert in espionage that enemies of the service or double agents often meet their ends in bizarre, startling ways: mutilations, injections, bodies in suitcases or odd sexual positions. Such curious arrangements have the effect of a diversionary jolt – impeding clear thinking by arousing fanciful speculation.

Naturally and persuasively, Joyce reminded us that she had interviewed Judith O'Donovan who had known key players in the drama. Judith testified how powerful and distressing was the experience of Jack Mossop's wife, Una, who had to put up with her husband's depression and hear his troubled description of the murder and subsequent disposal of the body. "The secret army was allowed to kill any persons who might be putting the country in jeopardy," Joyce pointed out. "An injection with a poisoned needle could bring on a heart attack."

Lacking contact with a living witness, I was impressed, and yet knowing someone does not authenticate the information they dispense. As Jack Mossop received medical treatment, it is likely he passed on the story elsewhere, and yet it was only Una who profited from it.

Surely, if she believed a murder had taken place, she was by then an *accessory* and should have told the police rather than a newspaper? Some men *do* confess to crimes of which they are innocent and police make lists of such types to prevent them impeding the course of justice. Still, Joyce's account *does* stand as the most authoritative explanation so far. Yet why did this sophisticated bi-lingual Dutchwoman dress like a cheap tart in poor quality clothes? Was this her undercover guise? Would putting herself around like that be likely to assist her in gathering top-secret information?

Knowing I was spending the next day around Hagley, David sketched a map of the scene of crime, marking it as close to the Hagley Wood Lane junction on the A456, only 25 yards in from the tearing traffic of Hagley Causeway. The following morning I left my room and walked down the even slope from the Badgers Sett.

Not far from the junction, I came across a trinity of large white snack vans, two parked on my side of the road and the other on the Hagley Wood side. I was feeling hungry but decided not to be deflected.

Crossing the road, I jaywalked between juggernauts and forced myself through a hedge. Then I leapt across a ditch and into some soggy grass. Seconds later, a proud and valiant trespasser, I was standing in the fastness of the woodland. There were big earth walls standing about as if an artificial hide had been erected by a nature watcher. Thick shadows cast by the tall conifers made the undergrowth appear sparse and silent.

Loitering among the boughs, I had a sense of displacement allied to a pang of ominous solemnity, brought on by a knowledge of what happened in the past. The original Wych Elm had stood nearby but had been hacked apart in order to extract the body. So I moved out of the trees into a patch of open grass, finding a lopped-off trunk standing up like a post, as if marking an event. If slightly creepy, the place was not frightening, the woodland having a managed, tidy feel. Notices warned of access being barred, and that it was an area set aside for police dog training.

I wandered back among the looming, doleful trunks, with their folds of green and grey shadow mingling with seeping shades of bark and slatted spears of light.

'Who Put Bella in the Wych Elm?' echoed in my head.

No answer, only nature going about its business – spreading green shoots over the defunct tragedies of yesteryear rather than bleeding afresh at each gory anniversary. It was a downcast place with an undertow of birdsong – but evergreens *do* emit a funereal feel. If Bella's memory *was* alive, it was not by dint of any throat-catching atmosphere, only through our legend-making propensities. Far from forgotten, the mystery of 'the corpse who never was' thrives, lately buttressed by tales of road ghosts that stalk the lanes and dual carriageways in defiance of science and rational rebuke.

Left:
Hagley Wood,
site of the
murder.

Below:
David Taylor,
graphic
designer and
parasearcher
& Joyce Coley,
historian.

THE SUSPICIONS OF SUPERINTENDENT SPOONER

Superintendent Spooner

The Walton Murder was abandoned rather than officially closed. To Fabian it was not so much a blot on his dashing career as an utter failure – an enquiry that slammed against a blank wall and spattered what little impulsion it had gathered in a mist of blood and supernatural babble.

In the mid-1950s, he had retired and, with the advent of television, his fame had peaked so spectacularly that he was granted a TV series to immortalise the thrilling cases of his career: *Fabian of the Yard*. "In the nation's war on crime," the narrator announced, "Scotland Yard is the brain of Great Britain's man-hunting machine. Routine, detail, science and tenacity, these are the weapons used by squads of highly trained men: men like former Inspector Robert Fabian, hailed by the press as one of England's greatest detectives!"

An American model was adopted that broke new ground. The storylines were 'real' and provided an insight into the day-to-day work of a London police detective. It was an interesting mix. The hurried urgency of presentation owed much to the hard-boiled, interior monologue style perfected by Raymond Chandler in his detective novels, but cut-glass, BBC accents dominated Fabian's series, save in the portrayal of rough-cut Cockney villains. The series showcased London as a city of glamour and intrigue: shots of Parliament, Big Ben and Tower Bridge aplenty, with black cabbies rushing by and slurping up the rain. Bruce Seton well-conveyed the lightning-minded detective and, at the close of each adventure, Fabian himself would appear and deliver a snappy little reflection – a mannerism later mirrored in *Dixon of Dock Green* when Jack Warner would intone his little homily at the close of each episode.

Ten years after the Lower Quinton Murder, Fabian brought out his best-selling memoir *Fabian of the Yard* and relished the glamour and publicity. Often he featured as 'talk of the town', touring America, appearing on over eighty TV shows and being made an Honorary Citizen of New Orleans. William Katz, the pre-interviewer for Johnny Carson, had Fabian flown over from England. The Inspector told Johnny about a period in 1930 when, as a young bobby, he'd patrol outside the home of Sir Arthur Conan Doyle who was slowly dying. It was his job to make sure no one made any loud noises along the gravel road.

Fabian apparently was the only guest in the history of the Tonight Show who, on being introduced, walked in the wrong direction – towards the band rather than Johnny. Katz recalled: "I wondered at the time how many clues he might have missed doing that as a detective." After the show, he fell into a panic because he could not find his trench coat – "a detective without a trench coat is like Barack Obama without a teleprompter."

The coat was found draped over a chair in the office.

Asked how to deal with the crime wave sweeping over America, Fabian replied "the cat", meaning the whip. "I'd have liked to see him go after Al Qaeda," remarked Katz.

As a retired dignitary, the abstemious, generally sensible Inspector decided a greater interest might be aroused in his journalism – his sporadic reflections and opinion pieces – if he stopped being a level-eyed, tenacious cop and started giving the public and newspapers a teeny bit more of what they wanted. If it be Black Magic, let them have it, black candles, goats and all. Switch up the heavy breathing, add some Voodoo trappings – tom-toms, naked writhing women, blasphemous tidbits – and, hey presto, London doubles up as the Devil's Capital!

This is the entrance to the Temple of Satanism. Inside the walls and ceiling are covered with magic symbols. Oil lamps, burning a dark green fat, give off a hideous smell, their purpose being, I suspect, to blanket the odour of chloroform or ether with which the room is sprayed. At the far end of the room stands the altar, like the ones you see in church, but with black candles on either side and an inverted crucifix hanging above it. Near the altar stands an idol from an African fertility rite, five feet high and obscenely fashioned. The worshippers rub it with their bodies.

Unfortunately the Black Mass was a grubby masquerade. Fabian had to book a seat for it, as if it were a night at the opera. Compared with the open butchery of the Walton Murder, it was a mere floorshow. In his list of dreadful escapades, the anecdotal value of the latter ranked high, being included in his case-study memoirs *Fabian of the Yard* and *Anatomy of Crime*. Evangelically, he plays up the black magic aspect, as if pitting himself against the forces of supernatural evil rendered him disadvantaged: thus he was absolved from failing to make a conventional arrest:

Charles Walton lies buried in Lower Quinton's peaceful churchyard; a murder victim whose killer Fabian of the Yard failed to bring to justice. I have never said this publicly before, but I *think* I know who did it. Who though will come forward with the evidence?

He is in effect saying: Who will dare to defame the name of John Alfred Potter, and yet boldly he adds:

A terrible aspect of the entire affair is that the murderer, whoever he or she may be, might still be at liberty and could kill someone else who strays into, or falls foul of, the coven's evil net.

This is not congruent with previous allegations. In discussion with Richard Whittington-Evan, Fabian indicated Alfred Potter to be the murderer. Yet if a witch was responsible, is he covertly attributing necromancy to that sombre countryman? Surely even he could not imagine beefy John Alfred, church sidesman, devotee of horse-racing and cricket, cavorting in a night-black negligee – or whatever witches wear – around black candles and pentacles. Potter simply was not a wand and broomstick person. No, he was more a castrating tongs or – indeed – pitchfork type.

111

THE VIGILANT CONSCIENCE

With Superintendent Spooner, the failure to solve the Lower Quinton murder rankled. It affected him more than it did Fabian – after all, it was on his patch. He stayed open-minded, paying close attention to any black magic yarn and tale of witchery that might offer a lead. Even if he was not likely to catch the murderer, he did not want to think of him sleeping easily in his bed while Charles Walton was rotting underground. So he inaugurated a campaign of mild intimidation that hoarded the implicit assumption the killer came from Lower Quinton. Like a vigilant conscience, each year, on St Valentine's Day, he visited the village, strolled around; sometimes he took a drink at the local inn and visited the willow tree under which the body of Old Charlie had lain. He would glance meaningfully at certain locals in hope of one them flinching or breaking down and confessing – but that never happened. Still, the visits provided good copy for the local papers, although some resented the intrusion. But the avowed hostility was also disquieting. Why did they not welcome the vigilant eye of a senior police officer? After all, it was likely this extremely brutal character was still on the loose.

"There may be a simple explanation for the crime," Spooner reflected. "But the motive could equally be a fantastic one. The villagers are frightened to talk. That was our trouble right through the investigations. I go to the village. I talk to people. I let myself be seen. If the murderer is about, he wants the crime forgotten, and this may wear him down. I don't need the file. Every date and detail is in my mind."

But in January 1964, following the death of Alfred Potter, Chief Superintendent J.H. Dodridge of the Warwickshire CID, observed that, with the passing of the chief living witness, there was little likelihood of the case being satisfactorily solved. "It is still open," he emphasised. "When we open files, we seldom forget them. It is some time since we had a new lead, but if anything does occur it will be thoroughly investigated."

LIKE A GILDED GHOST

As Superintendent Spooner had a little of the literary man in him, with his books on local history, it would be interesting to know whether he was cognisant of that celebrated pastoral autobiography *Cider with*

Rosie (1959) by the poet Laurie Lee which has an unsettling chapter entitled 'Public Death, Private Murder' dealing with country practices that may not pertain to the murder of Charles Walton but certainly throw light on the reticence of country folk in the 1940s and earlier towards anyone who aroused the hostility of the community.

Lee tells of how a young man from his village went away to New Zealand, made a large sum of money and, many years later, returned, tanned and purse-proud. He entered the local pub "like a gilded ghost, successful and richly dressed" and proceeded to taunt his ex-mates for being set in their ways and stay-at-home. He bought round after round of drinks which they accepted as he held forth on their cultural impoverishment. Meanwhile the weather outside was turning to blizzard and cutting snow and, when it was time for him to go, confidently drunk, he went singing up the hill to his lodgings. But before he got there, he found some young men waiting for him by the old stone cross.

"Well, Vincent," they said, and he stopped singing.

They hit him in turn, beat him down to his knees, beat him bloodily down in the snow. They beat and kicked him for the sake of themselves, as he lay there face down, groaning. Then they ripped off his coat, emptied his pockets, threw him over a wall, and left him... He didn't stir again from the place where he lay; and in the morning he was found frozen to death.

The police arrived, investigated and found out nothing. Just as in Lower Quinton, their enquiries were greeted with cold stares and sullen disclaimers. Eventually the detectives were forced to leave, the murder unsolved, but everyone in the village could name the young men who had done the deed.

"I saw them often about among us," recalled Lee, "simple jokers, hard-working and mild – the solid heads of families. They were not treated as outcasts, nor did they appear to live under any special stain. They belonged to the village and the village looked after them. They are all of them dead now anyway."

CHARLES WALTON'S POCKET WATCH

One late incident, however, did awaken rumour and expectation in Lower Quinton. The metal detectors that groomed the field in which Old Charlie had been working did not manage to find his precious pocket watch, only the white metal chain to which it was attached.

113

Of the watch, at the time of the Coroner's Inquest, Edie recalled: "Every night he used to wind it up before he went to bed and place it on the wash-stand beside his bed. I have never known him go about without his watch."

Edie goes on to say that it was a plain metal pocket watch, snap case at the back, white enamel face, English numerals, keyless, with a second hand and – if she remembered rightly – the name Edgar Jones, Stratford-upon-Avon.

Fifteen years later, in August 1960, during the demolition of outhouses behind Walton's former cottage, a workman saw something shining amid the rubble. On picking it up, he found it to be an old tin pocket watch. Later that day it was identified as the watch that Walton was wearing on the day of his death.

The police were keen to examine the watch, hoping for a fresh clue. Certain maker's marks were recalled as being inside the case. They appeared to be present, but the watch-maker himself was dead, so the police could not confirm it was the real thing. In McCormick's version, he discussed the watch with a local who spoke of a mysterious piece of glass that fitted neatly inside the case and was suppose to possess magical properties. "I couldn't see that it had any practical purpose," he said. "It was a black glass and what's the use of that? Not an eye-glass or dark lens, just a piece of ink-black glass, more like polished coal, except it was as smooth as glass, yet not quite like glass, if you understand me."

Noticeably, Edie never mentions this bit of witching-glass that is developed in detail by McCormick and subsequent commentators. Later Cecil Williamson strained to forge a connection between it and the celebrated obsidian crystal of Dr John Dee, the Elizabethan spy and occultist, a man who has come to the fore owing to his fantastical and impressive system of angel magic.

As for the graves of Farmer Potter and Charles Walton, they can no longer be visited. The murder attracted the attention of so many strangers that, after a while, relatives found their interest a little ghoulish, and the headstones were removed. "All I found," one enquirer reported, "was a very small, half hidden, stone bearing the initials C H W. There was no date and no other details."

THE WITCHES OF SAVEOCK

Many people readjusted their notions of antiquity after a wave of revisionist historical studies, stimulated by Ronald Hutton's *Merry England*, pointed out how many buoyant country festivals – alleged in some instances to go back to prehistoric times – were comparatively recent 'constructions'. The general line of argument was that most of the beliefs of Old England went out with the Dark Ages. Some leftover superstitions were sustained during the Early Medieval period, but by the coming of the Tudors only trace elements remained that were eliminated by the witch trials and other crackdowns. Some customs and celebrations may be traced back to William and Mary, but there is little chance of establishing an unbroken continuity. For the Protestant Interregnum had banned many as 'pagan' – later they were revived with the accession of Charles II and the 'relaxation' of religious persecution.

SINCE PREHISTORIC TIMES

Hence the anthropologist Margaret Murray was wrong-headed when she invoked the suppressed yet ever-potent religion of the Goddess as being kept up in secret hideouts since prehistoric times. Far from upholders of a faith or belief-system, witches were mere throwbacks to superstitious country ways, clinging to charms, curses and herbal remedies.

Hence, when I began writing on the Lower Quinton and Hagley Wood murders, I had no marked occult or witchcraft agenda. I did not think the covens of the 1940s were involved in either death. I took the view that the procedures of modern witchcraft did not come into their own until they had been developed and formalised by men like Gerald

Gardner. I saw witchcraft as an ancient concept that had been taken over and synthetically assembled in the post-war period. Therefore I tended to be dubious of theories claiming for it an ancient lineage.

Then, one day, I read an article in *The Times* by Simon de Bruxelles, reporting an archaeological excavations at Saveock Water, a valley near Truro. It described the finding of 35 pits dug into a clay platform of the Mesolithic age. Apparently birds and other creatures had been used for rites involving swan pelts, dead magpies, unhatched eggs, quartz pebbles, human hair, fingernails and part of an iron cauldron. The earliest pits dated from the 1640s, a period of insurgence and political change in Britain when there was great hatred of Catholics and any non-believer or 'witch' was liable to treated harshly.

The archaeologist heading the excavation, Jacqui Wood, is a leading authority on prehistoric cookery and metalworking, well-known for her hands-on approach. She had advised on the discovery of Europe's oldest human mummy in 1991, the "Iceman" recovered from an Alpine glacier, and was drawn to a practical rather than mystical rationale. Initially baffled that the finds were not backed by written or anecdotal evidence, she concluded the pits had a ritualistic or religious intent. After putting out numerous feelers and enquiries, she began to think no other site presented the same type of puzzle.

Saveock Water is a reclusive little vale huddled in a fold of hillside, past which stampeding herds of traffic barge into Truro and westwards towards Redruth and Penzance. Three streams meet there and it has a serene, magical atmosphere. Nearby hamlets and placenames – Salem, Threemilestone and Chacewater – blend peace, witchery, numerology and swanlore. The water from its well was prized as pure and unpolluted during the 19th century when the adjoining land was mined.

Apparently, in the 17th century, Saveock was little more than a community of five houses whose occupants worked at a nearby mill, but its historical lineage is spectacular. Human occupation of the site dates from the Mesolithic Period, some 8,500 years ago. A stone-lined spring that may have been a "holy well" was dug out and found to be full of offerings from the 17th century, including 125 strips of cloth from dresses, cherry stones and nail clippings. Afterwards the well had been blocked up, presumably to conceal what went on there.

Each of the feather pits was excavated and examined. Lined with the intact pelt of a single swan, they were about 40 cm square by

17 cm deep (15in by 6in) and contained more ornithological votives. A "leaf parcel" was found to be packed with stones traced to Swanpool beach, near Falmouth, and famed as a gathering place of swans. Jacqui Wood noted: "Killing a swan would have been incredibly risky at this time because they are the property of the Crown."

One particular feather pit yielded a macabre treasury: dozens of unhatched eggs flanked by the bodies of a couple of magpies – birds long-associated with witches and devilry:

It had the same swan feather lining and on either side were the bodies of two magpies and between them were over 55 eggs. The shells had dissolved, but the membranes were intact due to the constant spring line flowing from the peat below the clay platform. When we looked at them closely they were a mixture of eggs from different birds from bantam size to duck egg size. The most intriguing discovery was when we looked at the egg membranes more closely and found 7 of the eggs had fully formed chicks in them ready to hatch! It was suggested by someone when we found the eggs in the pit that it was some obscure sort of egg preserving pit! But who would preserve eggs by first killing a swan and skinning it to line the pit with, then killing two magpies (People in Cornwall are still very superstitious about harming magpies today) and then put in over 55 different-sized eggs with some chicks trying to chip their way out of them at the time!

Jacqui Wood observed how formerly she had tried to avoid a ritual interpretation for an unusual find, but this site was full of it: "You see," she explained, "a lot of the paganism of the Celts was wiped out by the Romans, but not in Cornwall. Swan feathers had a connection with fertility. It's possible these offerings were being left. Then, if conception took place, nine months later the person would return to empty the pit. Often, when secret rituals are abandoned people, will talk about 'things that were done in my grandmother's day' but there has been no whisper of this. It really makes me wonder whether that is because it is still going on."

Dating the pits revealed usage at a time when the law stated "thou shalt not suffer a witch to live". In the mid-seventeenth century, a public frenzy of burning, hanging and drowning erupted until people began to feel more doubting and 'guilty' about their original convictions, resulting in the retraction of the death penalty for witchcraft in 1735. The Swan Pit with the Magpies and eggs was dated from 1640s – 1680s. A hundred years later (1740s – 1780s) the Cat Pit was dug out and lined, indicating four generations of ritual use.

The Dog Pit produced startling evidence. Traces of bomb-carbon were found there – evidence of nuclear testing that went on through the 1950's. This meant the dog had been alive then and, incredibly, affirms over 350 years of use. More gruesomely, a Goat Pit was recently uncovered that dated from after 1960 – for it had plastic baling twine in it. The alignment was north-south and the imported "purple crystalline sand" covering the body was identical to that in the Cat Pit and the Swan Pits, dating from 1640 A D.

This suggests that, through the hectic changes of the Civil War, the Industrial Revolution and Atomic Age, a body of people were visiting the pits and practising a mode of reverence pre-dating Christianity by centuries. The veneration of birds, their attributes and magical properties, may be traced back to the early Celts and Druid priesthood. One finds Cornish saints befriending and feeding them like St Petroc who was kindly to all living creatures. The magpie in particular was a bird of portent and revelation.

The evidence gives credence to the notion of a tribe or group of witches or family of spell-makers who passed knowledge on to their children. Evidence was not continuous. Long intervals were not accounted for, but knowledge of the pits and their purpose was kept alive by the generations occupying the cottages.

A student from Exeter University, who was working on the Saveock project, visited the Red Lion at nearby Blackwater. In between drinks, he told the local people about the pits and the curious relics that had been recovered. He was startled to hear they all seemed to know that witches had been living in the area of the pits. They mentioned a man called Burnett who was thought to be a witch and lived in a cottage the other side of the railway line next to the site. He died in 1945, so he could not have bedded the dog pit as that came after the atom bomb testing. He left his cottage to his two nieces who, according to the locals, were witches too.

A footbridge ran over the railway line when the two sisters lived there – that is, until the 1960s, when it was demolished. This cut off access to the pits and quartz pools on the other side. Hence Jacqui Wood knew nothing about the sisters and their esoteric rites. "There is no way," she explained, "across the railway track to their cottage now and in the country, if you live on a farm and do not share a track with people, you rarely get to meet them." The sisters's nephew inherited the cottage around 1985 and presently lives there.

Set against this, Charles Walton's death may be re-framed and related to what little is known of beliefs and practices of witches in Warwickshire and the Cotswolds c.1945. Although the Saveock site is styled 'unique', it is not a freakish "one-off" as corroborative evidence has started to flow in from Germany and elsewhere. It underlines how the custom of animal sacrifice persisted in secret for hundreds of years despite war, social upheaval and industrial land-grabbing. It does a little towards re-instating the theories of Margaret Murray, showing witches like Hobbits living parallel with rural communities, tenaciously continuing their midnight practices, sometimes known to others, sometimes ignored or overlooked, into the Nuclear Age. The rites of Saveock – digging votive pits and lining them with furs and feathers – have more in common with the well-rites of the Bronze Age than the charms, crystal balls and orgiastic 'sabbats' of the stereotypical witch. In a sense it is 'wish-craft' rather than witchcraft as it is concerned with bringing about desirable outcomes for a small body of people.

A comparable stubborn isolationism may be found in Byron Rogers's portrayal of the coracle men of the Towy as a race apart, living on their strip of marshy land beside the estuary, ignored by landlubbers and the rest of humanity, so who knows if they also did not retain their own superstitions and practices? There may be more tiny riverside and estuarine communities of perhaps less than ten people, practising ancient beliefs with pits, birds, bones, shells and feather, carrying on something that goes back more than a thousand years before Harold died on the field of Hastings.

Can an archaic custom kept up for a long period in an obscure part of Cornwall uphold the massive burden of Margaret Murray's contentions? No, it certainly cannot, but what Saveock Water does spell large, is that there are practices that barely touch the culture of archives or leftover notes and diaries. Historians seek documents even when the living event is being enacted a few fields away.

Inspector Fabian & RAF Officer witch-watching at Stenness.

THE DREAM OF EUGENE ARAM

A propos previous chapter, if early witch rituals did persist into the 20th century, this does not necessarily illumine the death of Charles Walton or of Bella in Hagley Wood. It does not *prove* they had a ritual intent, but it does confer *credence* to the rumours that leftover pagan beliefs were kept up by a select few and *may* have had a bearing on the murders. Cut-off hands and bits of bodies were *thought* to be used by witches, but ordinary, callous killers, like the late Fred West, often mutilate for no clear reason; also using a pitchfork may be deemed ritual, but it is also *commonsensical*, a dangerous weapon as are other implements if misused.

In the instance of Bella, stuffing a body in a hole is far from rare. A famous crime of the 18th century, with relevance to both the Lower Quinton and Hagley Wood murders, is the slaying of Daniel Clark, who was killed by a scholar and teacher called Eugene Aram helped by William Flaxman, a flax-dresser. After relieving the "stammering, pockmarked and weedy cobbler" of £220, Eugene brained him with a pick, doubled up his corpse and squeezed it beneath a rock in St Robert's Cave, Knaresborough.

Knowing he had been seen in the company of Clark the previous evening, Aram decided to leave the district, going first to Nottingham and then to London, where he lived a full and profligate existence, until a yearning for academic life tempted him to take a post of teacher at the Grammar School in King's Lynn, Norfolk.

He was a stern and authoritarian teacher who performed his duties ably. But then, in June 1758, a Knaresborough visitor to the town recognised him. Aram was arrested but denied his identity. However, two months later, under interrogation, he confessed to the crime and led the Justices to the remains at St Robert's Well. For about a year, he was confined to York jail where he wrote an elaborate defence, pointing out the bones in the cave might be the relic of a saint or hermit – but this convinced no one. Found guilty, he attempted suicide by slashing his wrists the night before the execution and was dragged half-dead to the gibbet. He was publicly hanged at Tyburn Field outside the gates of York for the murder and his bones were left dangling in a nearby forest. Seventy years later, the grim and tragic affair was resurrected in Thomas Hood's black and swaggering ballad – stanzas often recited at Victorian musical evenings by another callous criminal, Charley Peace.

I know that murderers walk the earth
Beneath the curse of Caine
With crimson clouds before their eyes
And flames about their brain;
For murder hath put upon their souls
An everlasting stain.

(*The Dream of Eugene Aram* by Thomas Hood)

THE TREE OF DEATH

By giving voice, art cannot recreate the experience, only the part that inspired or moved the artist. In the instance of Bella, this has to be the pointlessness and sheer horror of her end. Judging from the state of the corpse, her slaughter was a crude, hurried affair. Margaret Murray hinted the hollow tree was selected out of all others, but more likely the murderer wanted to remove himself from the place of execution as fast a possible, so he stuffed the body in the nearest hole rather than one better-tailored to the corpse.

I doubt the crime was a result of long planning. It was far more like an expression of sadistic rage. It recalls the fates doled out to prostitutes or women who go along with men of a psychopathic disposition. The police thought Bella might be a refugee who fled to the forest in order to avoid the falling bombs in Birmingham. What seems equally likely is that whoever killed her had first taken or forced her into Hagley Wood – a known resort of lovers – and in that lonely place assaulted and mutilated her. It is quite possible that Bella innocently went along with his initial request. Little suggestion of a sexual crime was raised by the police investigation, and one asks why? Sex was long-established as the motive of many crimes, but Webster found no evidence of violence – not always an easy thing to pick out on a disarticulated skeleton unless there were cut-marks on the bone.

Today, with DNA testing almost standard, a rotted skeleton is a more revealing object than it was in 1943. Back then, a detective lacked an extensive computer database that would enable a full analysis and comparison of, say, a sex slaying accompanied by a savage mutilation of the body, with a similar attack in the past. With the advent of 'profiling', a modern detective knows far more about the psychological type who is likely to perpetrate such a crime – young, male and sexually immature, for instance. The severing of the hand and the forcing of the body in a tree would also pick up corresponding assaults.

As for trees, they are seen as friendly to man, offering shade, serenity and physical restoration, attracting campers and holiday-makers. Equally positively, the word 'body' has been translated as a play on 'Boddhi', the sacred tree under which Buddha found enlightenment. However, in Early Medieval times, forests were also judged dangerous places where robbers and brigands gathered. Something of this aura persists today, especially in woods and parks near major centres of population that tend to attract Peeping Toms, prowlers and those who choose to die by their own hand.

This is apparent from the world news. For instance, in Bavaria, the decayed body of a German man, who committed suicide in 1980, was found in a spruce tree, 40 feet above the ground. It had hung undisturbed for 29 years. The skeleton was bound to the branches half way up in the woods near Bruckberg and, like Bella's corpse, was found by a teenager exploring the area.

India, a continent that still retains an ancient tradition of tree-worship, abounds in arboreal tragedies.

A Kolkata, a 12 year-old girl was discovered hanging by the neck in a bamboo grove near her residence in the Nadia district of West Bengal. She was without clothes and six inches above the ground. "This is an incident of murder," the police said. "We can't say if the girl was sexually assaulted." Similarly, in New Delhi, the semi-naked body of a young woman was found hanging from a tree in a public park. "She might have hung herself with the sari she was wearing," a police official said. "She was only in her undergarments when we reached the spot." Likewise, at Kuala Kub Barus, the body of a young woman, thought to be a rape victim, was found dangling from a durian tree clad "in a white bra and maroon panties." Strangulation marks on the neck indicated a struggle.

There is also an example of forcing a body into a confined space as happened with Bella. Police in Greensburg, America, recovered the body of a 30-year old mentally feeble woman who had been stuffed into a garbage can in a school parking lot after being forced to consume detergent and urine and write a fake suicide note "before being fatally stabbed by attackers who shaved her head and painted her face with nail polish."

This makes depressing reading, and yet the point of itemising these crimes is not to smear the character of Bella, but merely to underline that her end *was* woeful and sordid. Time adds a tragic dignity, a venerable remoteness, that distracts from the visceral savagery. Hence the subject continues to lure aficionados who sojourn among the Unsolved Slaughters of Yesteryear. Why are people so taken up with the dreadful acts their own kind visit on their own kind?

THE IMPORTANCE OF FILTH

I gained an insight into this when I was a young and working for the Leisure Services on the seafront at Clevedon, beside the Bristol Channel. My headquarters was a big shed of a building called the Glasshouse and my boss was Bernard Faraway – a marvellous man and a joker. That morning, he had skimmed off a mass of frothy black seaweed from the morning tide and bundled it into a sack to feed his garden. When an elderly council worker called Harry arrived, whose job it was to attend the car park barriers, he saw the sack and started to pull Bernard's leg.

"What on earth d'you want that for!" he exclaimed. "All that muck and cadmium the tide's brought in, that old weed and scum from Cardiff and Swansea, why d'you want to dump that on your garden? It's filth, that's all!"

Bernard replied pleasantly. "Of course it's filth – don't you know anything, Harry? Filth's good for you. Iodine, salt from the sea, muck, scum and sludge, that's what makes things grow. Everyone needs filth to grow up strong and healthy."

I was amused and impressed. Analogically speaking, Bernard was using the argument of the eminent psychologist, Carl Gustav Jung, who split with his colleague, Sigmund Freud, after judging the latter's narrowly sexual reading of human nature did not allow adequately for the spiritual aspect. Jung maintained the filthy, dark, guilty material of the subconscious mind was also yeasty, fertile and potentially stabilising if 'integrated' with the everyday social self. If not integrated, it might form a separate strata that strikes out alone, as in a crime of passion.

A partiality for the disreputable is a universal character trait. People love to burrow into their lower reaches, to study dubious books, read about shameful, lascivious deeds, acts of greed, deceit and lechery. They hold a mirror to our secret selves, in that most men and women have urges that will betray them at some time or another – if only in a small way. Naturally they temper these, trying to appear as decent, reasonable citizens. But occasionally these urges take over. They surge over the breakwater and overwhelm whatever niceties and inhibitions may be there. When the deed is done, others look on with dread and fascination and from time to time condemn, but some, perceiving these acts as dreadful potentials in all of us, might mutter: "There, but for the grace of God…"

This applies to the Hagley Wood Murder that has sunk itself into the soul of the country around Birmingham. The very name 'Bella' exudes the baneful fascination of those wicked ladies the actress Margaret Lockwood used to play. The legend has become charged with a macabre lyricism, and today visitors trawl through Hagley Park and try to find the murder scene in the same way as they might check out the place where Harold fell on the field of Hastings.

Recently a short television film, featuring Joyce Coley and David Taylor and fronted by Angelica Bell dressed in a Sherlock Holmes hat and cape, was uploaded to U-Tube. In scary-frivolous style, it traced Bella's history and provoked a vitriolic online debate between a young woman, who expressed sympathy for the victim, and a man who replied: "What a dismal little moron you must be. Your violently obsessive ranting, demanding justice for murders – some of which

125

occurred over 100 years ago – clearly point to your needing psychiatric help. Your self-piety in the 'death of a young woman' is truly odd and your whacko suggestions 'perhaps the 4 young boys knew more than they were letting on', only back this up."

Clearly Bella is still potent enough to stir a latent friction and, though positive hopes for a solution have long expired, it remains 'open' and unsolved, falling under the jurisdiction of the West Mercia Police who regularly refuse access to the documents they have accrued. The murderer is in all likelihood dead and, though there's a possibility that (presuming he's male) he may have confessed to someone or recorded it somewhere, this seems less likely with each succeeding year. What keeps it active and charged is the legendary character it has accrued, the steady infusion of its diabolic mystique into the minds of succeeding generations.

On 18 August, 1999, a mild flurry of publicity ensued when the stone panel at the base of the obelisk crowning Wychbury Hill, on the estate of Hagley Hall, was scrawled with the long-honoured shibboleth: "Who put Bella in the Wych Elm?" It is not beyond the skills of a literate graffiti artist to inaugurate a dialogue but no one so far has chalked an answer and, of course, many would be curious to learn what possible one-liner could lay this to rest.

Badgers Sett – haunted by Bella.

THE LEGACY OF CECIL WILLIAMSON

Witchcraft Museum, Isle of Man

A character who interested Tess Kingham was the film-maker and intelligence officer, Cecil Williamson, who later turned into what may be called a Witch Collector General, going up and down the country, gathering charms, ornaments and artefacts relating to the old religion. Being something of an impresario, Cecil decided witchcraft had commercial possibilities not hitherto exploited. So he decided to classify his choice artefacts and put them on display in a museum. It was set up at Castletown on the Isle of Man after the Second World War along with a restaurant called 'The Witches' Kitchen'.

In 1947 Cecil invited Gerald Gardner to collaborate in the enterprise. Gardner initially joined Williamson and his wife – an 'honorary wizard' – but later moved into a house in Malew Street. With the repeal of the Witchcraft Act (1951), the business prospered for a couple of years, but Williamson wanted to pursue mainland promotion.

After selling the museum building to Gardner, he moved the collection to an old drill hall in Windsor and a pub called 'The Goswells'.

Although the venture was a success in its new location, prominent locals objected. Williamson was pressured to re-locate it to Bourton-on-Water where it again aroused opposition. Locals called it 'Satan's House' and "Christians" burned down a section of it.

Incidents of this kind drove Williamson's collection first to the little Cornish harbour of Polperro, and then, in 1960, to Boscastle where it still remains, despite the recent, ferocious flood. By then Williamson had entirely broken off from Gardner, judging him as "very, very vain, self-centred and tight with money…"

Cecil was born on September 18th, 1909, in Paignton, South Devon. His father was a career officer in the Fleet Air Arm of the Royal Navy. As a child, he claimed to have witnessed "a major public act of witchcraft" – an old woman being stripped and beaten by townspeople for allegedly using her skills. He tried to intervene on her behalf but to little effect. A few years later he picked up hints on retaliatory spell-casting from another old woman which led to a boy who had been bullying him having a skiing accident. From then on, wizards, warlocks and weirdos beset his path.

As a young man he attended Malvern College in Worcester (the academy to which Aleister Crowley had been sent), spending his summer holidays in Dinard, France, with his grandmother and her medium friend, Mona Mackenzie, who taught young Cecil clairvoyance and divination. When he finished his schooling, his father sent him to Rhodesia to study tobacco farming. But as his African houseboy – Zandonda – turned out to be a retired witchdoctor, he learned about Voodoo as well.

In 1930 Williamson returned to London and joined the film industry. After working as a production assistant for several studios, he met Gwen Wilcox, niece of film director and producer, Herbert Wilcox. Gwen Wilcox was working as a makeup artist for Max Factor of Hollywood and Cecil married her in 1933. Throughout his marriage his interest in the occult and witchcraft persisted, resulting in an expanding range of friends and academic contacts, notably the Egyptologist, E.A.Wallis Budge, the black priest, Montague Summers, and the anthropologist, Margaret Murray.

Obsessed by lore and ritual, Williamson collected more and more magical relics. "Witches and sorcerers," he told a reporter, "are no different from anyone else. They all die and have to have their effects passed on. So you hear about this, and off you trot up country, and you are taken into the magician's den, and you pick up what is to your liking. But I am conscious that everything has a spirit or soul. The first thing I do with a piece is to put it in a room I use quite a lot and get to know it, find out whether it's a spirit bottle or not a spirit bottle – though you've only got my word for it, quite a lot of the exhibits can be unstable."

After the debacle on the Isle of Man, Cecil returned to the Cotswolds, where he continued to clear out houses and manors in search of relics of witchcraft and ancient superstition. This was in preparation for setting up a new Museum of Witchcraft at Bourton-on-Water. A place in the area of special interest was Snowshill Manor, near Broadway. "A most sensational magician's den," was his verdict. "I went there after the house had been taken over by the National Trust. It belonged to a Mr Wade whose family fortune had been made in sugar in the West Indies, and he knew quite a bit about Obeah (Voodoo). The National Trust architect discovered the outside measurements of the house were different from the inside ones. Well, there was a secret room which no one knew about, and I was called in to clear it."

This mysterious upper room was inscribed with a pentagram and furnished like the laboratory of a medieval alchemist. Charles Paget Wade (1883 – 1956) was a noted eccentric, collector and benefactor, who counted among his friends Virginia Woolf, John Betjeman, John Buchan and J.B. Priestley. He acquired the rambling Cotswold mansion of Snowshill after the 1st World War, so that he might use it to house his ever-growing horde of artefacts. Practical, obsessive and fond of dressing-up, Paget was certainly open-minded and intellectually curious enough to try his hand at spell-casting, although many of the stories his secretive personality attracted – that, for instance, he was werewolf as well as a master of the black arts! – are fallacious.

In an email, Tess Kingham commented on Cecil's role at Snowshill:

I have a photocopy of the picture Cecil Williamson took on entering the 'magician's den' at Snowshill if you are interested. The [Boscastle] Witchcraft Museum has info on the clearance and what was found. It's grim reading – human tallow hand-shaped candles, etc. I'd love to do an expose of all the National Trust and other august 'heritage' properties that have dodgy occult pasts like Cardiff Castle. Somehow this info never finds its way into the tour guidebooks.

The murder of Charles Walton obsessed Cecil, and he usually traded the same explanation for it. Tess Kingham went through many of his articles and papers, gleaning what she could. "I looked into the big houses," she reported, "from whence Cecil Williamson claimed the order went out to kill Walton because he had overheard something."

What was Cecil's big secret that he cogitated over in his place of retirement, The Mill House in Fore Street, Tiverton? Alone and enwalled by grisly, stomach-churning relics, he composed rambling, spirited and rather repetitive letters and articles to Michael Howard, editor of *The Cauldron* – a lively, informative periodical on folklore and witchcraft.

I can still recall the events of that February in 1945. The War was drawing to its close. The US troops had broken through the Siegfried Line and the Russians had taken Stettin. I was back at my MI6 base at Whaddon Hill close to Bletchley Park. Just before going into lunch, Brigadier Gamber Parry stopped me and said, "Oh Bill, here's a bit of news that should be of interest to you. There's a report out of a witchcraft-style killing of some person, not so far away from here, and I thought you might like to look into it."

So Cecil takes a journey to Lower Quinton, finding the place awash with newspaper men. The locals were hiding behind their front doors and keeping their mouths clamped. Having picked up the basic details of the crime, Cecil asked a farmhand in what way was it connected with witchcraft and the answer he got was: "Well, yum don't heave a body like that, does ee?"

Cecil enquired: "Like what?"

"Well like them say, all fancy like."

Cecil returned to base very little wiser. He had been recruited for the MI6 by Lieutenant Colonel Edward Maltby who wanted him to gather names, locations and interests of persons actively engaged in the "high upsurgence of occultism" in the German Reich after June 30th 1934: The Night of The Long Knives.

Maltby was deputy-director of Section VIII of MI6. His job was to produce wireless transmitters and radio networks for SIS agents working abroad. He was related by marriage to the occultist, Dion Fortune, whose magical partner in her pre-war *Fraternity of the Inner Light* had been Colonel Charles Seymour, also an SIS officer, who was later appointed head of the Dutch section of the SOE. Cecil Williamson's role at Bletchley was to supervise mobile radio stations in Southern England broadcasting 'black' propaganda to German U-boats patrolling the North Sea and the Atlantic.

Years later, the war over, Cecil finds himself back in Gloucestershire and the 'magical' Cotswolds as sole owner and presenter of the Museum of Witchcraft at Bourton-on-Water. The place has proved a supreme attraction. Crowds are flocking to admire the implements and images of folklore and superstition. But one day, a man asks why he has nothing on show relating to the murder of Charles Walton.

He replies: "I know nothing. You tell me."

Cecil is told to go to a chemist's shop in Shipston-on-Stour, a village that apparently has a witch buried at one of its crossroads.

He follows the advice, contacting the owner of the shop who tells him this story of the Lower Quinton murder.

Back in the early 1930s, in the Vale of Evesham, which embraces Lower Quinton, lived a well-to-do fruit grower. Owning a large house in the catchment area of his business, he was well-educated, but his learning was scholarly rather than rural. In fact, he was a student of occultism whose special interest was the magic of Dr John Dee (1527–1608), Mathematician, Secret Agent and Astrologer Royal to Queen Elizabeth. Midway through his career, Dr Dee teamed up with a man who is often classed as a crook or trickster, Edward Kelley, who assisted him in his mystical transcriptions.

At a testing juncture in their shared magical career, Kelley declared that he and Dee should swap wives in order to fulfil the orders of a certain spirit. A notable item of Dr Dee's magical toolbox was his celebrated black obsidian *shewstone* that may have been a black polished mirror rather than a crystal ball. It was used to facilitate many a demonic or angelic communication that came through in decorative and resounding phrases: "I am the daughter of Fortitude," went one, "and ravished every hour from my youth…few or none that are earthly have embraced me, for I am shadowed with the Circle of the Stone…"

Briefly this wealthy fruit-grower set up an occult group, comprising men and women, whose aims were to duplicate and take forward the work of Dr John Dee, looking into the future, performing Enochian rituals (referring to the magical tongue he devised) and generally trafficking with souls of the departed.

"This happy state of affairs," Cecil declared, "was terminated by the declaration or war in 1939." The group shut down, each member taking up their wartime duties. This marked the entry of Charles Walton into their lives. Apparently the wealthy fruit-grower knew Walton as a man who could be trusted to safely store his precious stone during the period of disbanding. Conscious that Walton might seem an odd choice of protector – especially as the stone could easily be placed in a safe – Cecil explains:

Bank safes are not spiritual, and what is wise for mortal man is of little use in dealing with the world of the departed. Hence a living spiritual keeper was required and Charles Walton was selected for the job of Keeper of the Stone, being the key to the door between the two worlds of Here and Hereafter.

Cecil hovers a bit, adding more John Dee material before firmly appraising the character and tastes of the murdered man. He presents Charles Walton as a working class man of limited education who had "exceptional skills" in a number of rural crafts, as a horse whisperer, a toad talker and a bird charmer – all bordering on the supernatural. He was in demand from the farming fraternity and liked by most but was "shocking stubborn".

In 1943/44 the fruit and vegetable merchant died, but his occult legacy was taken up by two females who revived the order. Their duty, as they saw it, was to salvage from the estate all documents and magical implements that formerly belonged to the group, so that they could pursue their studies with the proper equipment. One piece they wanted in particular was the small black obsidian stone given to Charles Walton. They made contact with him and asked him to hand it over, but he refused.

Over the months he put forward various reasons for his refusal, but would not budge. Eventually tempers started to fray. A ceremonial ending for Walton was duly planned for St Valentine's Day. Cecil reminds us that, early on the morning of the murder, two persons on horseback were seen, one a female of about 30 years riding a grey, and the other a man of about the same age on a brown horse.

This is a rather fantastic preamble, drawing on McCormick and newspaper accounts, but amid the meanderings, some pertinent observations stick out: that the murder may have been committed by two persons – a notion that has never been raised. Yet Walton's forensic report indicates he struggled vigorously with his attacker and,

132

were there two present, one would imagine his arms would have been firmly held in place and there would have been less traces of cutting and bruising.

Much of what Williamson says is easy to dismiss, for he is adept at placing himself at the centre of intriguing situations. Yet he was also a wide-travelled collector who had seen remarkable sights. Though able to spin a yarn, he did appreciate veracity and, as Tess Kingham pointed out, British Intelligence deemed him an asset:

People who knew him often say that Cecil Williamson liked to elaborate and 'spin' stories about his work for MI6 during the war. However, as an MP I had access to the House of Commons library researchers and tracked down some of Williamson's 'Whaddon Hall' experiences. I discovered he was a trusted figure with some authority in the secret intelligence units (SOE and PWE etc.) working in black propaganda linked to the occult, and he was pals with many key intelligence figures such as Sefton Delmer, Wheatley, Fleming, etc. He undoubtedly knew Crowley's circle, not forgetting Crowley's extensive German occult contacts. Williamson was tasked to investigate these occult societies.

Tess goes on to allude to Switzerland as the hub of a counter-espionage circle with links direct into the Abwehr and the possibility of a conspiracy behind the murders:

I have a very strong hunch there's more to all this…than simply occult stuff and spontaneous murders. I'm not one for conspiracy theories usually but after working in Parliament (I was on the strategic arms export committee!) I've got a feel there's a bit more underneath all this. It could all be smoke and mirrors but if so there's some odd coincidences in a very small geographic area with a relatively small group of people. (Don't forget too the 'Bella in the Wych Elm' murder in 1943, just 40 miles away from where Walton was killed. There are clear occult and secret service links here too – the case files are not made public and the autopsy reports etc. and many files mysteriously disappeared).

RELICS OF THE DEPARTED DEAD

Cecil had several stories about Charles Walton affecting the day-to-day life of his Museum of Witchcraft. He had a place put by for what he called 'Relics of the Dear Departed Dead'. Apparently he once received six "problem artefacts" or items related to suspicious deaths or acts of violence.

He gave them what he called 'The Jesus Treatment', lavishing on them love, care and affection. The first thing to do, he says, is talk to them, establish friendly contact, while the second stage is to quell their agitation so that they may rest in peace. By way of this accomplishment, he came across a number of intriguing if alarming items, among the most remarkable being when a man entered the museum and handed him "the alleged weapon that entered the naked belly of Charles Walton with great force, so much so that the upright thrust caused the sickle blade to emerge and to protrude through the bones of the ribcage."

According to Cecil, years after the murder, the police returned Walton's trade tools. His sister did not want them, and this man obtained them for his own obscure reason, disposing of all but the sickle. But he began to be troubled by a succession of lurid nightmares that would not go away. Charles Walton's soul was on the warpath, he believed, there was no rest for him until he found a satisfactory solution. And so, in due course, the man presented himself to Cecil:

So there he stood in front of me holding something wrapped in a far from clean bit of cloth. When unwrapped, it revealed the two sections of the long skim and slender broken fagging hook. The wooden handle had long since rotted away in the earth. My first thought was: "Well, how much is he expecting me to pay him for this hearsay relic of a man's death?" I did the fellow a grave injustice. Indeed, he would have willingly paid me to take the beastly thing off him. So I was left standing holding in my hands a rather grubby bit of cloth and two sections of a broken sickle blade. The poor chap mumbled a few broken words then turned and beat a hasty retreat from the entrance hall of The Witchcraft Museum.

This again is lively – quite funny in a macabre way – but surely that particular tool, being used as a murder weapon, would be retained by the police as *evidence*. In the same letter [21/2/95] he refers to his collection of occult documents and attempts to set them in order:

Since November I have made a start in sorting out my mountain of witchcraft data that include boxes of paper work, press clippings and letters reaching back to 1934. Yes, I am a hoarder – never throw anything away. Every day I surprise myself rediscovering data on long-forgotten witchcraft and occult incidents. Well, I am nearly at the end of the storage dump boxes. Next stage to re-sort and file under subject matters such as toads, active wayside witches, herbs and plants that kill and so on. Next problem, what to do with it?

In an earlier letter [6/12/94], Cecil supplied a pen-portrait of himself in his last years:

My wife is long-dead and my in-house, one time typist is in a Masonic Retirement Home. So I am now to type myself and live a hermit's life in a rambling old house. Thank God I have always been domesticated and can do, can cook quite posh four course meals. Right now, I am busy sorting out the mass of occult items held in store, such as Aleister Crowley's Baphomet ring and his seven-demon headed stick and also quite a number of items from Dr Gardner's coven at Brickets Wood near St Albans. Yea Gods, I could fill a place twice the size of what I have got on show at Boscastle. Yes, it is a bit of bind knowing what to do with the stuff as my daughter has not the slightest interest in any of my six different subjects. Anyway, not to fuss. When I am gone it can be put to auction!

A final piece of wisdom:

For my part I have always been interested in obtaining answers to simple questions. Such as: Is Death final, yes or no? If No, then what? In my long life, my quest has led me into many strange situations and to meet with many extraordinary persons. What do I do with the answers when I get them? Good question. Answer: Keep Them Under My Hat and use them to help me on my way to the next world.

Naturally, with Cecil's death, the documents did pass to his daughter who disposed of most, retaining for auction the collection of artefacts. The Witchcraft Museum at Boscastle managed to preserve and retain some of his papers where they remain in archive.

CECIL MEETS THE BEAST

In *The Talking Stick* (1993) Cecil provided an account of his dealings with Aleister Crowley whose seven-headed demon stick he had obtained from the scholar, Professor Thomas Higham, who had met Crowley at Oxford – possibly at the *Book of Thoth* exhibition – where he purchased the relic from the near-broke magician.

A few anecdotes follow that are definitely dubious, styling the ghastly sacrifice of a cat at Cefalu a publicity stunt and having Crowley admitting to Cecil that his densely disquisitional magical tomes with their rituals and tables were all bluff.

Crowley instantly agreed. "You have hit it my lad. It was a big con."

(This seems an unlikely admission from a magician whose each book was a testament of faith. Crowley took a great deal of pain over the design and preparation of his sacred texts, employing magically appropriate colours for the binding and sympathetic astrological correspondences for the date of publication – making every effort to launch them effectively.)

Cecil then introduces his former partner, Gerald Gardner, who came over to England from the East, "running around like Wee Willie Winkie" in search of magical knowledge. He did not get on well with Montague Summers who was a Catholic, but secured a more satisfactory relationship with Crowley who allowed him into his magical organisation, the OTO, providing him course details which the other rapidly absorbed, apparently ascending the grades. Gardner soon became tired of paying Crowley for his tuition. "It is getting very expensive," he complained, "and what I have seen up to date is a load of rubbish."

Briefly Gardner left Crowley's order, taking with him two of the magician's paintings were given to Gardner in exchange for a silver ornament. One was of a naked woman in the middle of a mountain scene which Cecil put on display in his earlier Museum of Witchcraft in the Isle of Man. Eventually a police inspector came along and asked if the painting meant anything. He was told it was the work of the Great Beast or wickedest man in the world, and the inspector enquired: "I'll tell you what, down in the toilet, what paper do you use?" Cecil told him that he used a brand called Bronco, a roll of which was handed to the inspector who cut a tiny bit from it, making a miniature sporran which, with the aid of a tiny bit of glue, was stuck on the offending anatomical feature.

CONE OF POWER

More relevant perhaps is Cecil's account of the operation to repulse whatever psychic force the Nazis were harnessing for their cause. Cecil was sent to Ashdown Forest that was then under the control of the Canadian Corps. His brief was to locate a site "for an enormously powerful radio station" that had the code name 'Aspidistra'. Moving into a small building at Chuck Hatch called Gorse Cottage, he started requisitioning land for the project, contacting the farmer and offering compensation.

Then he heard from the Brigadier the MI5 were getting together a group of people for "a sort of pantomime set-up" in which England's foremost "wizards" delivered a ritual curse on Hitler and the Nazi regime. Obscurely, he added, it had to take place on the South Coast because the Duke of Arundel was hosting as guests "two of the top nuncios from the Vatican" and the Vatican was in "close cahoots" with the German High Command who were deeply into astrology or prediction.

It was decided this "Curse-Hitler" or "Stop-the-Invasion" ritual should be held in the forest. Aleister Crowley and his son, Amado, were invited to oversee the proceedings. Amado's job was to sit in a chair with a big mirror in front of him and behind him a dummy figure representing Hitler, all of which was enacted next to the estate church. The Fire Brigade was present and about forty Canadian soldiers who did not wear the normal uniform but were draped in dark grey army blankets over their heads, so that they resembled monks. To liven things up a little, the Canadians took a little initiative of their own, adding mystical signs and decoration to these somewhat drab robes.

Cecil goes on to evoke the climax of this bizarre military masquerade:

The high spot of the whole show was that, having done a certain amount of ritual nonsense, Crowley's young son Amado did the final things in front of the mirror and then, who-oo-oosh, the figure of Hitler was pulled up to the top of the church tower where it was taken out of the cradle and put onto a long rope, running to the ground. The dummy figure was ignited on top of the tower, and when it was blazing nicely, it was allowed to run down the wire. It was not a very successful run because the cable had a bit of a dip in it! Anyway, it flamed up and set fire to the bushes, but the fire brigade was able to put them out. And then the soldiers went home and everybody went home.

As for the operation Cecil portrays, its provenance may be traced via Dion Fortune down to his one-time colleague, Gerald Gardner, who described how, in a clearing near the Rufus stone in the New Forest, on a warm night at Lammas (August 1st), his own and other covens gathered to draw down the same 'Cone of Power' that had (allegedly) helped wreck the Spanish Armada and repulse Napoleon's attack.

In the summer of 1940, the Cone was needed. A payment to the gods was necessary in order to harness the full thrust of its spiritual

137

potency. To launch this mystical missile, a sacrifice was necessary. It is said two of the oldest, feeblest witches volunteered themselves for this risky rite. Apparently they offered their bodies which had to remain 'skyclad' and unfed while the others smeared themselves in weather-protective grease, as they chanted and pranced in a circle, attempting to kick-start a massive energy vortex from the ground. In this way, they would be more likely to catch a chill and die, boosting the efficacy of the operation by literally giving up their all.

This is how the *Book of Shadows* puts it:

Imagine now that whatever energy drove the circle to turn against the ground has burnt through it and now is *turning the ground inside the circle* (as you stand on it). Imagining the world turning around you should be easy after spinning in place. Imagine the world turning around you as smoke rises from the burnt circle on which you imagine yourself standing. Imagine the smoke swirling around you, up to eye level and then over your head until it reaches and meets at a single point directly above your head. Imagine the smoke moving faster, picking up speed. Allow it to speed up until you feel the need for release of the emotional tension. At this point you can recite the final spell to manifest your desires into reality.

Regrettably two of the older witches did pass away after the series of rituals against invasion had been conducted.

"Although the details are a little sketchy," a writer commented, "the magical power came from the people themselves. In some way, not fully explained, this force was formed into a cone, which could be directed at the mind of Adolf Hitler. Cynics will scoff, but history records that there was no invasion."

ENHANCING ONE'S HORSE APPEAL

One can easily grasp why MI6 made use of Cecil's skills in intrigue and storymaking. He is very definite about names and details. You are sure he has been to the place he evokes; the minor details seem right, like the dip in the cable, but surreptitiously a colourful, inventive element has been painted in, like the Canadian servicemen in their bizarre monks' robes and the wasteful deployment of the fire brigade for what was only a masque.

Cecil ends his article on Crowley with a chirpily salacious anecdote that demonstrates his facility at 'improving' or upping the comic content of the original. John Symonds, in *The Great Beast*, mentioned Crowley's use of what he called his sex-appeal ointment that made horses in the street neigh appreciatively:

"Outside the Piccadilly Hotel, I think it was, that Crowley told me that he had a formula to make a particular pong by mixing all sorts of herbs and oil, that would make any woman who got a sniff of it to fall over backwards, rip her knickers off and say, 'I'm yours!' So, for good measure, he dressed up in a Cossack uniform with astrakhan hat and these cartridge things on the front, with big lapels and shiny boots, drenched himself in this new-made pong and strolled out into the street where there was a United Dairies milk dray with the usual small pony that drags it. The milkman was missing. Crowley steps onto the pavement, looks left, looks right. The United Dairies pony curls its lip back, goes ne-e-eigh and belts up the street and turns the entire truck over. Bless his heart, he could tell a story like that against himself. I liked him."

Again we are impressed by the specific detail, the name of the hotel, the stage-managing and special effects, and then, at the climax, human warmth breaking through, the good-natured salutation of a decent friend to his old pal. "Bless his heart…"

One cannot take offence at such frolicsome asides, but because Cecil is never mentioned in Crowley's diaries, it seems unlikely these hilarious episodes were either witnessed or confided. In fact, after sampling his recollections and those of Amado Crowley, I thought they were both suffering from a defect in their veracity filter, arising from a complaint which I shall call *empathalitis*, a coinage derived from 'empath' or 'to sympathetically identify with another' and 'itis' denoting an illness or inflammation.

From time to time, I have noted in certain individuals a disposition that may be characterised as extreme enthusiasm with certain aspects of your experience. If ever you confide a remarkable happening, they can find an experience to match it or exceed it in brilliance and colour. At first you think, they are telling the truth and say to yourself, "Well, well, what a widely travelled, well-informed and versatile person Tom is, what a life he has led."

And then, at some point, Tom will make a claim that cannot be true, like being present at a historical event witnessed by only one person, and you do not care to challenge him, call him a liar because he is not really that, but an ardent, buoyantly amiable self-deluder, an ostensibly candid, sincere fellow, whom you do not want to damn or demoralise. Thus you tactfully file him in your brain as one suffering from empathalitis.

Cecil Williamson, like many others, had read John Symonds's lively and culturally influential biography of Aleister Crowley (*The Great Beast*) and was enthralled by the bizarre richness of anecdote, spectacle and magical lore contained therein. Indeed it was landmark work that fascinated where it might have been expected to shock. It galvanised Williamson so that he regretted not making an effort to contact Crowley when he was alive, and so, to find out more, he wrote to Gerald Yorke, a former disciple.

After all, he told himself, I was at times so very close to him. I knew occultists and witches who had crossed paths with him and on many occasions must have been only a hair's breadth from a physical encounter. I deserve to have known him – I have a *right* to have known him. And so, bit by bit, into his writings creep these pantomime reminiscences, largely filched from the lesser anecdotes of others. The same is true of Amado Crowley who selected a father who would best suit his emerging self-image, a combination of blatant rebellion and diabolical glamour.

REFLECTIONS ON RITUAL SACRIFICE

SACRIFICE ON THE TECHATL STONE.

Aside from folk festivals and ceremonies attached to the agricultural year, rituals might be defined as sacred procedures by which we dignify life's thresholds: birth, marriage and death. They are set up to assist, celebrate and make memorable these transitions, so in a sense a ritual killing is an anomaly, a vanishing act rather than a ratification of a stage of growth. In early civilisations like the Babylonian, horrors like child sacrifice were practised and animal sacrifice was routine. In Britain, the Druids were reported as constructing huge wickerwork figures in which they placed their prisoners or 'enemies' and afterwards ignited. The horror of the image shivered down the centuries and passed into English Literature:

It is the sacrificial altar, fed
With living men – how deep the groans! the voice
Of those that crowd the giant wicker thrills
The monumental hillocks, and the pomp
Is for both worlds, the living and the dead.　　(Wordsworth: *The Prelude*)

Owing to the erosion of belief in a personal God, sacrificing one's life to a greater principle – as, for instance, Muslim terrorists attempt – is translated as a gesture of fanaticism. In this century, such an act is regarded as worthless and ineffectual, for death implies absence from the arena of existence. Though a fatality may produce a wave of after-effects, it is not regarded as a reliable tool to generate a definite outcome.

If people are going to make life-sacrifices, it will tend to be soldiers who will be paid and taken into account for their services to the country. For those, however, who sacrifice themselves to an unknown god, little sympathy is offered, so few being able to identify with such an intensity of conviction.

In analysing ritualistic murders, it is pertinent to recall the fate of 'Netta' or Marie Norah Emily Edith Fornario, a member of the Alpha et Omega Temple, loosely affiliated with the Golden Dawn. On an afternoon in late November 1929, her naked body was found on a hillside on the 'holy isle' of Iona, off the western coast of Scotland. Where she was lying was a Fairy Mound to the south of Loch Staonaig, an area rife with superstition and magic.

Around her neck was a blackened silver chain and cross – near her hand was a large steel knife or ritual dagger. The latter had been used to cut a large cross into the turf on which her body was lying. Netta had been running for some distance before arriving at the mound as the soles of her feet were torn and had bled a great deal, although the heels were unharmed. Her death certificate stated she had died from "exposure to the elements and heart failure". She was buried by the islanders of Iona on the following Friday.

Netta was born in Cairo in 1897, only a year before her mother, Mrs Norah Fornario, died in Christchurch, Hampshire, aged 33. Her father, Guiseppe Fornario, was an Italian doctor. After his wife's death, Dr Fornario returned to Egypt, leaving his daughter in the care of her maternal grandfather, Thomas Pratt Ling, a wealthy tea dealer, who was of a firmly Protestant disposition. When he died, aged 73, his will specified that his granddaughter, Marie Norah Emily Edith Fornario, would receive £12,000 provided that she married a Protestant man who was not one of her first cousins; furthermore she must be a UK resident living in the Protestant faith. If she did not follow these instructions, she would only inherit half the money.

Judging from her grandfather's blatant opposition to his late daughter marrying a Catholic, friction arose between Ling and Guiseppe Fornario. This may have been passed on to Netta who developed an animosity towards her father. An excitable young lady, artistically advanced but difficult and edgy, her personality was carried along by impulsive fads and rushes of psychic inspiration. After her grandfather's death, subsisting on a private income, Netta dressed with a flourish – a tasteful ostentation characteristic of the arts-and-crafts style. Her garments cleaved with her body's mould rather than sought to constrict. Long hand-stitched silk or wool tunics were her preferred mode. Her hair alike was arranged in two heavy plaits. She never wore a hat, possibly because she thought a fine head of hair provided the necessary defence from the elements.

A friend of the occultist and 'high priestess' Dion Fortune, before setting off for Iona, she had been living for some years in London, at Mortlake Road, Kew, with Mrs Varney, her housekeeper, who told the press that Miss Fornario did not believe in doctors and thought people should cure each other by healing waves or positive mental vibrations. Mrs Varney found Netta generally cheerful, if erratic and inclined to experiment at times, once launching into a 40-day long fast that she sensibly abandoned after a fortnight.

In August or September, 1929, Netta set off for Iona in order to take forward her occult studies. Accompanying her was an impressive mound of luggage "containing enough furniture to equip a small house" and implying that she intended to stay for a long time.

Her landlady on Iona was Mrs MacRae who ran a guest house called Traymore. Soon after moving in, Netta captivated her by her knowledge of healing and spiritual matters. Mrs MacRae listened as the intense young woman told her she had recently been in a trance that lasted a whole week. Naturally this worried Mrs MacRae. It was her job to oversee the comfort and happiness of her guests, but having to pay close attention to one in a zombified or bewitched condition was rather stretching her remit as landlady. Mrs MacRae became anxious. What if Netta was unable to shake herself out of it? Netta replied that, under *no circumstances*, should she call a doctor.

Beautiful, desolate places do not instantly yield their secrets. Netta roamed the empty beaches, sacred shrines and ruined habitations of Iona, hoping for insight. Apparently she was an adept in "green ray healing" that invokes the energies of Archangel Raphael to neutralise diseases of the mind and body. Was she trying to cleanse herself or the spirits with whom she claimed she was in contact? Iona was seen as a place where the veil between the temporal world and the spiritual was tissue-thin. An invisible portal was sited there, allowing the mystic to step through and explore the hidden reaches. The problem was to locate it. She climbed to the high point of Dun I and had an entrancing view of the island, set in a shock-cold emerald sea, with silver sands and tiny bays, and visited the steep rocks of Cnoc Druidean where the pagan priests had enacted their rituals. In the evening, she would resume her trance state, hoping the island's spirits would breathe their secrets into her soul. She wrote to Mrs Varney at Kew an obscure note warning: "Do not be surprised if you do not hear from me for a long time. I have a terrible case of healing on."

One Sunday morning, Miss Fornario was up very early, and her manner was troubled. She told Mrs MacRae that she had to leave for London immediately because "certain people" were threatening her by telepathic communication. Her gist was not easy to follow, especially when she invoked "a rudderless boat that went across the sky" and voices from beyond.

This alarmed Mrs MacRae who noted that Miss Fornario's silver jewellery had turned black overnight. But no boat was available for her return, for it was a Sunday. So Netta gathered and packed her belongings. The practicality of all that effort must have soothed her. A reversal of mood followed and, later that day, she announced to Mrs MacRae that she had decided stay on Iona indefinitely.

The next morning Mrs MacRae entered Netta's room to find it empty. This did not worry her, as she had become accustomed to her moods, but when most of the day passed with no sign of her, she began to fear for her safety and wandered along the moors and beaches. About two and a half miles away from the cottage were the remains of a village in which Netta had expressed interest, though she had never visited it, as access was difficult. It was within half a mile of this village that her body was found.

Soon after the recovery of the body, strange stories circulated in the Western Islands that told of flickering blue lights observed near her body and "a cloaked man" in the vicinity. Letters of "strange character" were also received and "removed" by the police, who passed them on to the Procurator-Fiscal for "consideration", but these were wraiths of speculation that never got anywhere.

Netta's lonely death, along with the complicated mysticism of her character, perturbed her friends and added a tragic dimension to the island. The official verdict was that she had died of cold and exposure when the balance of her mind had been upset. The fact that she was naked under the cloak suggested she had hoped for some profound spiritual experience – many regard clothing as an obstacle to such transmissions. She had carved the large cross in the turf with her own ceremonial knife and lain down in it, hoping that it would protect her from whatever risk she was taking.

Lady Garrote, after researching Netta's background in some depth, thought family conflicts in her early years had left her feeling unloved and that she may have decided to become a healer to compensate for the wounds suffered back then. The Green Ray and the 'little people' filled the gaps that her family in their coldness had overlooked. Furthermore, she speculates that, being born in Egypt, Netta was better able to apprehend the occult mysteries than the other members of the Golden Dawn who possibly begrudged her superior insight.

If so, little evidence of Netta's spiritual hardihood was apparent on Iona. A sinister end like hers might be thought out of place on the sacred island of St Columba, but Iona's association with witchcraft long preceded the arrival of the holy man. The death of Natholocus, King of the Picts, was foretold by a famous witch who lived on Iona. Apparently her magic was highly effective, causing a rot to enter the mind and, even after the setting up of Columba's mission, there were tales of demons and imps spoiling the milk and wreaking mischief.

Such elemental, water-locked places, harassed by the hissing of the wind and the wash and withdrawal of the tide, can both reinforce an individual's resolve or wear it away like water does rock. Loneliness may strengthen the spirit but it can also disturb and disorientate it. Netta brought to the island no practical knowledge, no defining craft or occupation, only a rather neurotic mysticism, and that's, when all's said and done, not much to feed the troops. The isolated self loses definition and may end up overwhelmed by an inflowing surge of misery, depression or malign intention. Hence we read of stark suicides and bloodcurdling, violent crimes on lonely Alpine passes and thinly populated tundra regions where life is so harsh and toilsome one would scarcely credit there was time for such gruesome outcomes to take seed, let alone flower.

Dion Fortune suggested Netta set sail on an astral voyage, leaving her body behind. This recalls those stories of South Sea tribes who dream so profoundly they sometimes expire in their vivid adventures – or do they slip into an alternative reality that lays claim to them, just as travellers may be kidnapped by the countries who are hosting them? Because she was preoccupied by folktale and traditional enchantment, a story was extant that Netta longed to enter the

145

underground kingdom of fairy or 'faery' like the Reverend Robert Kirk who studied Divinity at St Mary's College, St Andrews, and became minister at Balquhidder and Aberfoyle before vanishing into Fairyland *circa* 1692.

In *Psychic Self Defence*, Dion cited friction with occultist Moina Mathers (head of the Alpha et Omega Temple of which Netta was a member) as an alternative cause. This is unlikely, but even today murmurs of conspiracy persist:

Netta went to Iona, a small Inner Hebrides Island in Scotland, to clean the place of bad vibes, but a mentalist lunatic probably got hold of her and killed her, leaving her naked on a turf cross, either to revitalise the island or to rid it of supposed witchcraft. The islanders closed up tighter than a clam. Netta Fornario had a rushed burial in November 1929, a few months after arriving on Iona from London. No real investigations were done into her death... It's obvious she was bumped off and all sorts of fairy stories concocted to hide the truth.

Francis King conceded the likelihood of Netta suffering from a 'magical attack', though he admits most people will think of her as suffering from schizophrenia and delusion. In one of her published articles, a review of the composer Rutland Boughton's ambitious spiritual opera *The Immortal Hour*, Netta refers to malign spiritual agencies:

The chorus of intuitions now gives place to a chorus of demons symbolising the dark atavism of the subconscious forces which endeavour to acclaim the abstract mentation as part of their own evil, because the reaction of the lower principles to the mistranslated stimulus of the super-conscious frequently produces disastrous results on the material and lower emotional planes. This is why Dalua is said to bring madness and death, which generally result from misapplication of metaphysical forces.

What is being said is less than transparent, but it could be translated as those who choose a life of the mind – preferring to live on a plain of abstraction – lay themselves open to demons. By ignoring or 'spiritualising' the claims of the body and the senses (what Netta dubs "the lower principles") they create an imbalance and weaken their psychic defences. Netta subjected herself to deprivational disciplines in order to enjoy a fuller life of the mind, but that aroused subconscious predators who tormented her. Jung's advice to Netta might have been to recognise the demons as parts of her that needed to be 'integrated'. John Layard, a student of Jung, might have pointed out her depression was based on "withheld knowledge" or hiding from what she knew about herself. A present-day physician, quite possibly, would have attempted to modify or balance her brain with drugs.

YOUR AVERAGE COUNCILLOR

The death of Netta Fornario had elements of intrigue but did not suggest a murder so much as a sad, lonely and deeply troubled act of self-sacrifice. Until recently, I dismissed the malevolent side of occultism, knowing killers have added pentagrams and symbols to their scenes of crime, usually as a ruse to throw off course any investigating detective.

If I heard of a so-called satanic or witchcraft murder, I tended to attribute it to a media source, a film or popular 'shocker' in which such themes are rife, rather than a rooted traditional belief or world view. Organisations like the Golden Dawn hosted academics, vegetarians and people who wanted to communicate on a 'higher plane'. Hence I tended to frame people who were interested in paganism as being greener and gentler than the rest of the population. I imagined all those dark rumours were exaggerations fanned by a culture of horror films and a morbid interest in diabolism.

So I did feel a jolt of shock on hearing of a murder that took place not far from where I live in Cornwall. It concerned finding adrift in a boat the battered body of a 56-year-old parish councillor of Budock, Peter Solheim. Floating in the open sea, five miles south-east of Black Head on the Lizard in June 2004, he had been drugged and mutilated by a machete or axe before dying from drowning.

The police discovered Solheim was the son of a Norwegian sailor. After a period of depression and mental illness, he had become a councillor as well as a notable member of the Druid and pagan sects, with a special interest in the Norse gods. In his house they rifled through hardcore pornography, grimoires, books of spells as well as a box of potions. There were many works on cursing and malevolent magic. He seemed to be drawn towards the menacing figure of Odin, a god of mutilation as well as thunder. Apparently he had suggested to the local council that Odin had a hand in the heavy floods affecting the community.

147

The irony is that, despite his baneful spell-casting, it was not Solheim who turned out the powerful one, but his diminutive, tubby mistress, Margaret James, 58, of Porthoustock, who planned his assassination to avenge his sexual treachery. He was seeing another woman, and she decided to curtail his pleasure. Co-conspirators were enlisted to oversee the murder, convey the bulky body into a boat and launch it into the sea. But Margaret refused to reveal their identities and they were naturally reluctant to step forward and supply details. Hence the Dark Wizard turned out a victim of the betrayed Mother Goddess. And there was no need for spells or chants to eliminate him. Just like the Roman army, Margaret favoured a solid, old-fashioned cutting implement. Poor Solheim. If there's one god to avoid aggravating, it's Aphrodite.

Sinister as it was, the Solheim murder was a crime of jealousy. If the trappings were unusual, the motive was commonplace

FLOATING IN THE THAMES

Far more terrible and pathetic was the report [28 Jan, 2002] of the dismembered body of a young boy found in the River Thames. Using an artist's impression, police sought information on this victim of a 'Muti' killing – a murder associated with Africa and witch doctors.

The boy, wearing orange shorts, was of Afro-Caribbean origin and aged between five and six. A Scotland Yard spokeswoman provided an artist's sketch, hoping to jog people's memories. The child was spotted floating in the Thames by a man walking across Tower Bridge on September 21, 2001, and had been in the water for up to 10 days. Police found seven half-burned candles wrapped in a white sheet washed up on the southern shore. A name – Jo Fola Adeoye – was written on the sheet and the name Fola Adeoye inscribed on the candles.

The forensic detective christened the boy 'Adam' and a reward was offered for information leading to his killer's conviction. They contacted police forces in Germany and Belgium where three similar cases have emerged, involving the murder and disposal of children whose bodies were placed in running water.

The Metropolitan Police consulted a South African academic, Dr Hendrik Scholtz, an expert on witch doctors, Muti black magic and ritualistic murder. He considered Adam's murder consistent with Muti

148

killings. The human parts were used as sacrifices to Muti deities in return for physical advantages: "the eyes to give the power of seeing into the future; the arms for greater strength; the legs for greater mobility; the penis, a particular prize, to give greater virility and fertility."

This type of killing, involving the trading for profit of human body parts, arouses horror in the West. Prejudice is liable to surface, a typical comment being: "Many people are unaware of this side of the 'noble savage'. It seems dabbling in human parts whether turning them into powder to make 'magic' or eating them is something noble savages excelled at until the evil whites stopped them."

Similarly the idea that Muti magic "epitomises the African way of thinking" and that one "can't move forward in life without destroying another's life." This is an audacious generalisation, a more charitable view being that, within the scope of a continent acclimatising to democratic notions of civilisation, throwbacks or barbaric practices are still common just as are they are in the remoter parts of Europe and Asia.

These three examples of deaths with ritual overtones point to a derangement and single-mindedness that is typical. Do they shed light on the Walton murder? Netta died within a carved cross, and Charles Walton had that symbol slashed across his neck (though not provably through design). Solheim's body was battered in a savage, haphazard way and placed on the sea as if to hint at a boating hazard, but the motive turned out to be jealousy operating within an occult framework. Spells were not involved, only brute force. The young boy, Adam, was closest to a satanic sacrifice, cruelly mutilated and donated to the river god. Like Solheim, his body was recovered from water and subjected to a post-mortem.

The use of sharp blades allied to a functional ghoulishness was a feature of the Walton and Bella slaughters (to which convincing motives were never assigned) only the ritual specificity does not fit easily into the rural communities of Lower Quinton or Hagley. At the time of Alfred the Great, such a slaying would have been considered barbaric. Could there *really* have been active in the middle of the 20th Century a belief system that decreed such a fate?

ON THE RAMPAGE

Thomas de Quincey, a connoisseur of opium and a leading writer of the Romantic period, wrote a celebrated essay, half-playful and half-macabre, *On Murder Considered as one of the Fine Arts*. It is rightly considered a minor masterpiece, though somewhat occluded by a verbose obliqueness – too many meaningful ripples distract from the current of argument.

Briefly De Quincey seeks to compare murders from the point of view of the effectiveness and skill involved in the execution. His justification is that, once a murderer has been condemned and the demands of morality satisfied, the seriously involved student will be drawn to compare narratives of the different cases, the degrees of finesse or brutality involved, and then to pass an aesthetic judgement. He cites Mr Howship, author of a book on indigestion, who shows no scruple in referring to a certain ulcer as "a beautiful ulcer", so why not be prepared to acknowledge merit in certain criminal acts? De Quincey is here playing upon the divide between 'beautiful' as an aesthetic as opposed to moral epithet: a 'beautiful' murder signifies the act was successful within the scope of its intentions rather than an alluring spectacle.

Aside from murder, other negative events arouse curiosity and elation. De Quincey evokes the appeal of wanton, disorderly acts of destruction, like the terrible fire which occurred at Liverpool docks, when flakes of blazing cotton were carried by the wind some eighteen miles eastward and "public sympathy did not at all interfere to suppress or even check the momentary bursts of rapturous admiration, as this arrowy sleet of many-coloured fire rode on the wings of the hurricane" – capturing the uneasy mix of lamentation and exuberant nihilism such things engender.

There is much impish argument of this type, interspersed with deeper reflections, where De Quincey identifies the release of power and intoxication which murder may confer on both criminal and spectator. As civilians rather than combatants (we tend to accept the legitimacy of soldiers 'killing' for their country), we place the murderer in a special class, for he has relinquished sacrosanct restraints:

Coleridge, whom I saw some months after these terrific murders [the Ratcliffe Highway murders], told me that, for *his* part, though at the time resident in London, he had not shared the prevailing panic; him they affected only as a philosopher, and threw him into a profound reverie upon the tremendous power which is laid open in any moment to a man who can reconcile himself to the abjuration of all conscious restraints, if, at the same time, thoroughly without fear.

THE RAGE OF ODIN

In recent years, a French sociologist has attached to the Norse deity, Odin, a wave of largely pointless, brutal assaults that are presently a feature of our society.

In connection with this, I recall an incident that took place along the Oxfordshire stretch of the Ridgway, an upland prehistoric route crossing Southern England. I had just passed the massive green terraces a glacier had cut out thousands of years ago on the flanks of White Horse Hill and, opposite it, Dragon Hill with its chalk scar and mysterious flat summit like a landing pad. Up by the Horse itself, it was so hot that sheep were seeking shelter in the trench of the figure.

151

Going up over the carving, I joined the prehistoric track and headed for the chamber tomb of Wayland's Smithy – a vast green longship of a sepulchre with massive upright sarsens guarding the entrance. It had started off sunny, but the sky was rapidly darkening. There was a hint of cold injecting the air and the leaves of the big beech copse enclosing the tomb started to rattle at the first drops of rain. I spoke to a Norwegian couple. The man was very amiable and holding a pole with a camera planted on top – a device he used for photographing crop circles. He had made his own diary, meticulously dated, with colour photographs and diagrams of all the circles he had visited. I praised his stamina and application, but as we spoke the weather turned. A blast of rain with a strong wind behind it pushed between us. He and his wife made off in one direction and I headed for the path leading to the car park.

Wayland hailed from Odin's pantheon. This was his domain, a place of ash groves and windy cemeteries where the old gods held out. Abruptly the rain became intense. The chalk path on which I was walking turned into a series of overflowing puddles that merged into a yellowish swirling stream. The path was babbling along like a shallow river. I took refuge in a copse on my right and stuck my back up against a trunk to shelter from the cold wet drops sweeping in shawls over the downs. The next instant there was a flash of lightning. The rain hurtled down, fat, quick-pattering drops, as if a waterfall was pouring through the trees. A moment later it was dark again, and I looked through a gap in the foliage. A red flash like a bloody eye winked at me – a jagged fork of fire needled down, following by another deluge. It was intensely dramatic. Odin – or, at least, his stormy compatriot, Thor – had decided to rattle the complacencies of Sunday strollers and tourists. The thunder god was out there, lobbing spears of lightning alternating with freezing rushes of rain.

Meanwhile a couple had joined me under the shelter of the trees. They were holding a baby whose cot was soaked and who was crying loudly. Knowing the rain had set in, I hurried back to the path and started making my way to the car park. I noted a vast elaborate corn circle in the field beyond the copse that seemed to have 'appeared' new-cut like a topiary exhibit.

I thought of the area thousands of years back when there was no road, no shelter, no accessible settlements or route of escape from a storm. It was over an hour before I got back to the car and about two hours before I thawed out. The German philosopher, Heidegger, sought to warn us against "forgetfulness of being" or failing to shiver with awe and gratitude at life and its marvels. Well, I'd forgotten how cold rain could penetrate to the bone like that. Although I'd tramped through intervals of thunder and lightning in the mountains of Norway and Switzerland, none had been as intense as that storm over White Horse Hill. It reminded me that, even in the temperate clime of England's chalk hills, nature could express itself in a wild, whirling and violent fashion.

A week or so later, I found myself brooding on Odin more searchingly. My mind went back to a book I had reviewed a year or so earlier by the popular historian with a vaguely radical slant, Richard Rudgley. It was called *The Pagan Resurrection* and it singled out Odin, assessing the cultural stamp he had made both in his native Scandinavia and on subsequent generations in Europe and America. Oddly enough, the English were never attracted to this wild, wayfaring and often malevolent trickster-god. Our literary visionaries and magicians tended to be sun-cultists, like D.H. Lawrence and Aleister Crowley, drawn to France, Greece, Italy and the myth of the Great God Pan who, in his Dionysian incarnation, possessed a similar fascination to Odin, standing for mystery, magic and trance states of lust and battle fever.

Rudgley touched on these aspects, tracing Odin through writers like Bulwer Lytton, author of that supremacist fable *The Coming Race*, and R.S. Tolkien who lamented that Britain did not have a national mythology like the Iceland sagas. Emphasis here falls on the Germanic notion of *volk* which goes deeper than the gentler English 'folk'. Rudgley's preoccupation was with a side or mask of Odin that had been sieved through the minds of various 'Aryan' apologists, notably C.G. Jung who wrote authoritatively of archetypes, translating them as deep-seated, dangerously eruptive racial tendencies that could be awakened by particular states of affairs – like, for instance, the appearance of Hitler in German politics after World War One. Basically his thesis was: Beware of this mad, bad, dangerous god! When Odin stirs in the soul of Germany, her neighbours had better look out for storm and thunder.

Halfway through, Rudgley brisks up his argument by introducing the French sociologist, Dennis Duclos, who, in *The Werewolf Complex*, scoops up Jung's argument and transplants it to America, claiming Odin has instilled himself in that volatile mega-culture, shape-shifting into innumerable wandering rapists and ultra-gruesome spree killers who behave like Vikings on the rampage. We are treated to the case history of a particularly murderous duo to illustrate Odin on the prowl:

Odin the horseman or the attacker is also the god of dangerous marauders…Helmeted like a Hell's Angel…he wanders his path in search of people to cast spells on, animals to hunt, misfortunes to inflict on others, wars to wage, or women to abduct. Odin…is also the god of the secret paths that lead to hell. Route 1-35 is such a path and, since Toole and Lucas travelled it, it could be renamed Helvegr, 'the road to Hell' in the Ancient Germanic language.

This is stirring, malevolent stuff – a teaser for a superior horror film. Unless we look out, Rudgley warns, the Odinist strain in human nature may spell the death of liberalism. He concedes there's a good side to Odin as well – green, meadow-fresh pagans prancing through woodlands and urging in needful ecological policies – but that has not yet come to the fore. Hence we should stay alert if we're not to be overrun by a counter-culture of free-ranging murderers and looters.

In my review, I was respectful as well as mildly disparaging of Rudgley's thesis. I thought the wider international application ill-timed, issuing esoteric warnings about a Nordic god while the Western World was cowering under tables fearful of Muslim terrorists. After that, I did not think much about Odin until the dramatic storm by the White Horse. Still later, my impression was reinforced by reading a profile of Peter Solheim who was obsessed by the Norse gods.

"He became very taken by the gods Odin and Thor and was veering towards the dark side of magic," recalled Tamsin Parish, a 23-year-old Druid who met Solheim in the late nineties. "Odin and Thor are Nordic gods, very powerful, and we were all worried that he might tap into that power…" Peter Petrauske, high priest of a Falmouth coven, added that, while the rest worshipped in plain white robes, Solheim wore a horned helmet and breastplate and carried a sword. "He told us he wanted to be known as Thor's Hammer."

It sounds as if Solheim might have been a fun guest at a party.

For myself, I decided that, if unable to shed light on the Lower Quinton and Hagley Wood murders, I might at least thicken the darkness – *diversify* rather than *clarify*. Much as in the attacks cited by

Rudgley, the notable aspect of the Lower Quinton murder was its sheer bloodthirsty abandon.

Were it a ritual, one might have expected a more methodological approach, but it displayed all the rage of a Ripper-style slaughter. Hence the date of the crime might be irrelevant along with the coincidence of the Black Dog and the mention of Walton in Reverend Bloom's work of folklore. This would literally be a crime without point, save the crude gratification of blood-spilling or a tiny sum of cash if Walton had any in his money belt.

Numerous precedents exist, demonstrating a violent intrusion followed by a gory devastation, and then a vanishing act. But I think in particular of the village of Monksilver, near the Quantock Hills, a charming place of cream-painted cottages with thatched bonnets and names like Meadowsweet and Limewalk. The church is endearing, too, with its Norman tower and lively gargoyles; only in the graveyard is a tomb bearing this inscription:

Inhuman wretch, whoe'er thou art
That did commit this horrid crime,
Repent before thou dost depart
To meet thy awful Judge Divine.

This is addressed to the unknown psychopath who murdered Elizabeth Conibeer, aged 88, and her two daughters, Anne, aged 45, and Sarah, aged 43, in the hamlet of Woodford, 5th June 1775. The family were going about their everyday business when a malevolent slasher entered, hacking and tearing into them so savagely that instantly the room was running streams of blood in all directions. The murderer was never found; no one had any idea who it could be. An inexplicable, mindless ferocity had erupted amidst the rural calm and instantly made away, leaving no hint, only the dreadful carnage.

If I invoke Odin, it is only as a way of evocatively pigeonholing a type of crime. For I am not *yet* crazy enough to attribute to a Norse God a couple of homicides, especially when a forensic psychologist, after studying the morass of stab wounds, would snap out a stereotypical profile: male, young, deviant with a short fuse. Only I *am* assigning a concept, an ominous swiftness, a wayward frenzy, a flip and careless attitude to death-dealing – 'like flies to wanton boys are we to the gods' – by supplying a mythological lineage. For Odin does, in a sense, belong to the area in question. He was very much a god of

Middle Earth – some cite Meon Hill as the original for Tolkien's Weathertop Hill – and the Kingdom of Mercia.

Over the fruitful Vale of the Red Horse, he looms in the legendary outline of the lost Horse of Tysoe or 'Tiwaz', a kinsman of Odin whose hand like Bella's was amputated. Even after settling into the identity of a stolid, Saxon farmer, Odin's old self would erupt in stabbings, witch-hunts and acts of needless sacrifice.

In a sense, the Walton Murder and Hagley Wood killing could be termed as acts that sourced barbaric techniques of dismembering, allied to an implacable rage that could be summoned to dispatch friend or foe alike. The sacrifice, of course, is enacted not for the benefit of harvest or crops, only to eliminate a human irritant or gain a surge of morbid adrenaline. If possessed by bloodlust or frenzy, Odin springs like a tiger rather than broods like Hamlet. I do not see either as a ritual killing in any procedural sense, more as uncontrolled, free-ranging, vicious attacks. However, if anyone wants to stream along with the occult symbolism – sacrificial date, pitchfork impalement, cross-shaped slash, spilt blood, black dog, severed-hand and tree-trunk grave – they'll find plenty for the taking.

Thinking about Odin and his attraction to corpses and violent endings, I recalled this passage from Brian Branston's *The Lost Gods of England*:

If a West Saxon farmer in pagan times had walked out of his *bury* or *ton* above the Vale of Pewsey some autumn day, and looking up to the hills had caught sight of a bearded stranger seeming in a long cloak larger than life as he stalked the skyline through low cloud; and if they had met at a gallows by the cross-roads where a body still dangled; and if the farmer had noticed the old wanderer glancing up from under a shadowy hood or floppy brimmed hat with a gleam of recognition out of his one piercing eye as though acclaiming a more than ordinary interest, a possessive interest, in the corpse; and if a pair of ravens had tumbled out of the mist at that moment, and a couple of wolves howled one to the other in some nearby wood; and if the stranger had been helping himself along with a massive spear larger by far than normal; and if all this had induced in the beholder a feeling of awe; then he would have been justified in believing that he was in the presence of Woden tramping the world of men over his own Wansdyke.

This disruptive northern deity insinuated himself into the mind of Robert Fabian.

At the end of the war, an RAF squadron leader told him that, when stationed on the Orkneys, he had become drawn into a witchcraft group who gathered for their Sabbat on Midsummer Night at the Stones of Stenness, twelve miles from Kirkwall. In the small hours, he had witnessed a girl tied to an altar and a goat being sacrificed. He had joined in the chanting and singing, and it was only later he noticed that somehow the skin on his left thigh had become branded by a triangular tree-shape, enclosed in a circle: the sign of Odin, supreme God of the Vikings who settled on the islands. He showed Fabian the mark and intimated the group was still practising. Intensely curious, Fabian agreed to go to the Orkneys with the squadron leader to witness the ritual.

So, around Midsummer, the two took a journey to the far north and spent a couple of wet, cold, misty days hanging around the standing stones waiting for the coven to manifest – but nothing happened. So rather disconsolately, they went back to their hotel rooms and the airman called: "Come and look at this!" Fabian entered and saw placed in the centre of the pillow on the bed a triangular black flint arrowhead: the sign of the Tree of Odin.

Fabian may have seen the sign, but only those who followed after were able to divine the meaning. It was a message to a cop of the old school, saying a new god was ascendant, a god who presaged the era of the New Anti-Christ, the random slasher whose act worships itself. It was of little use countering such madness with the patient methodology of the 'Hendon Way', repeatedly trudging back to the crime scene for further clues, for likely as not, the culprit was already over a hundred miles distant, poised to perpetrate yet another meaningless barbarity. Like Odin on the battlefield, he wallows in a boiling fury of destructiveness.[7]

This suspended threat is part of the heritage of Charles Walton's murder. The very air of the parish of Lower Quinton is darkened by mention of it, and I doubt if many inhabitants would feel completely at ease today, nearly seventy years later, walking down a dark lane alone

---

[7] Norwegian extremist, Anders Behring Breivik, showed similar fanatic fervour when, in July 2011, after detonating a truck bomb outside government offices in Oslo, he went on a shooting spree on Utoya Island, killing 69 young people.

or standing in a solitary field beside Meon Hill. And the same applies to Hagley Wood where Bella met her end. What happened back then is held back from us. No one was ever caught, arrested, hung or placed in an asylum. Hence, in a sense, these killers are still out there, wandering the dawns of our imagination, feeding off the fear they generate. In all likelihood, both are dead by now and were accorded a respectable burial. But as we shall never know, their spirit has proven stronger than their theoretical demise. In our minds, they are still on the prowl, loose and threatening – far more so than those locked in Broadmoor or Durham.

These unsolved murders, hanging over quiet country villages and towns, are rendered perpetual by the open verdict that energises their potency. They are similar to the 'nameless horror' of which Arthur Machen wrote in his tales of sorcery and sinister infiltration – a shapeless evil force that can flow into any crack in the skull, any fault-line of the mind. Without reason or accessible plot, they are akin to some mighty violence that hangs forever unrecompensed, an assault on existence itself, the echo of their infamy never being contained by force of law, logical solution or handcuffed felon. No, they are not to be tidied up and put away, but remain hovering in the air above that field, beside that well, in that quarry, landfill site, flooded cellar or derelict yard, infusing the spaces demarcating their origin and merging into folklore and – if possessing the right morbid enticement – the tourist industry. They hint to us that we shall never be truly safe. Somewhere, somehow, one consequence or another will seek us out.

The small stone, inscribed CHW, that's thought to mark
Charles Walton's grave in St Swithin's churchyard.

CULTURAL ECHOES FROM AN ATROCITY

*Pear-pickers surrounding 'Shakespeare' for the gruesome
finale of 'Afore Night Come'.*

People living apparently conventional lives and then breaking into extraordinary behaviour is a favourite theme of novelists and scriptwriters. Shy, secretive souls who murder or go on the rampage confirm Freud's theory of sexual or emotional suppression. What's more, if they decorate their homicidal antics with voodoo rites or something equally chilling, then the results add up, more often than not, to a lethally commercial combination. Hence the gruesome currents of the Walton and Bella murders, with their ritualistic symbolism, carved ravines into British culture, flowing into the imaginations of poets, artists and dramatists.

Reasons for this are easy to find if not especially trustworthy. By the mid-point of the 20th century, there was a decline in utopian visions, such as those anticipated by men like Bernard Shaw and H.G. Wells.

The atomic bomb and other ominous accomplishments stood in the way of people believing mankind was moving towards a perfected vision of itself. World War Two demonstrated a massive, orchestrated violence, added to which was the horror of the Nazi death camps. Formerly judged culturally progressive, the German nation had relapsed into barbarism and, granted the wrong type of leader, there was nothing to stop others from going the same way.

The theme of humanity crumbling into chaos and nihilism was taken up by novels like *Lord of the Flies* (1954) by William Golding, showing well brought-up British schoolboys stranded on a desert island and reverting to savagery. Earlier, back in the 1920s, T.S. Eliot's landmark poem *The Waste Land* and Edith Sitwell's *Gold Coast Customs* sent forth similar barbaric echoes. Partly inspired by Sir James Frazer's *The Golden Bough*, Eliot's masterwork braided anthropological, medieval and classical veins of learning, showing decadence and luxury side by side with various barren, painful scenarios: buried corpses, dry bones, dismemberment, rape and drowning. The mix of savagery and apathy in the poem hinted at a culture that had lost it way. Furthermore the novels of the period, especially those of Evelyn Waugh, followed suit, dabbling larkily in cannibalism and other tribal partialities.

'RITUAL' by DAVID PINNER

Eliot was writing sacrificial dramas at the time of the Bella murder, elements of ritual slaughter being present in *Murder in the Cathedral* and *The Cocktail Party*. Possibly he hoped such sensational touches might inject an authentic Jacobean chill into his placidly subtle blank verse.

A less canonical literary work, inspired by pagan-style murders, was David Pinner's *Ritual* (1968), a detective story blending grimness of subject matter with a jaunty staginess of presentation. Although the author utilises the classic props of 'folk horror', there is also something of a poet and rationalist comedian in him. The story is set in the Cornish village of Thorn where the dead body of an 8-year old girl, Dian Spark, has been found by an oak tree, clutching a sprig of garlic in her hand. The question arises: Is this a ritual killing? A brisk, practical police officer, Detective Inspector David Hanlin, arrives from London

160

and begins an investigation that is not noticeably hampered by the dark glasses he wears to protect him from sun blindness.

The reader accompanies Hamlin at his interviews with village notables, starting with Reverend White who insists the village is a Christian one, but the Inspector notices the altar cross is missing. The Reverend tells him it often vanishes and comes back. Hamlin later identifies a monkey's head and garlic flowers on the altar, inspiring the admirably bizarre rebuke – "Who would dare, during my angelical reign, who would dare place a shrunken anthropoid's head on my high altar! This is really removing Lucifer's trousers."

Another character the detective questions is the decidedly camp Lawrence Cready who manages a museum of witchcraft at the former manor house of Squire Fenn. He styles it as a collection put together for historical interest, but later Hanlin comes across a group of local children playing. A doll falls out of a boy's pocket that has a pin stuck in its abdomen and the name Dian written across its back. The child, nicknamed Fat Bill, breaks down on being questioned about this, yet admits that he hated Dian and that her mother is a witch. Soon after, Fat Bill is found dead by the same oak tree.

The story culminates with Hanlin being asked by Cready to attend a moon-worshipping ceremony held by the locals. He goes along and finds Cready clad in female attire while other participants are dressed as birds, horned creatures and march hares. The rite ends gruesomely with a white horse being sacrificed by the shore. But these sensational events shake up the revellers, loosening their tongues and providing Hanlin with a vital clue that identifies the killer.

Ritual stimulated the scriptwriter Anthony Schaffer to do something on the same lines for Hammer Films. The outcome was *The Wicker Man* (1973), now regarded as an eccentric classic, though it contains few examples of outstanding acting or filming.

The film was confidently directed by Robin Hardy and later dubbed "the Citizen Kane of British horror". It is a curious movie, blending black humour, heartlessness and a flouncy, Playboy eroticism. Sergeant Howie (Edward Woodward) travels from the mainland to a remote Scottish island to investigate a missing schoolgirl. On arriving at Summerisle, the upstanding, puritanical Howie discovers that the locals, including the schoolchildren, indulge in shameless sexual behaviour and are oddly indifferent to the disappearance of their former companion. Summerisle, lauded over by Lord Summerisle (Christopher Lee), turns out to be a fascist hive of hedonism. The islanders are locked in an idyll of bookish, over-literal paganism that distresses the bible-bashing policeman.

As Howie determinedly uproots and exposes their weird practices, he becomes convinced the missing girl has been offered as a sacrifice. But he fails to register that the tables are turning against him and that he is being selected for a similar, dreadful end. The final image of the ominous wicker man, whose flaming entrails are set against the cold western ocean, has burned itself into the public imagination and the accompanying music has a drubbing, mournful finality.

AFORE NIGHT COME

If the Celtic enthusiasm for burning was demonstrated by *The Wicker Man*, the equally horrifying practice of disfiguring and dismembering the body is well-represented by *Afore Night Come* (1962), a play by David Rudkin that owes its inspiration partly to the Walton murder. Rudkin was the only child of a devout pastor who denied his son and Irish wife such worldly pleasures as cinema and theatre-going. At school and later at Oxford, he studied the tragedies of Shakespeare and the bloody, incestuous dramas of Sophocles, Aeschylus and Euripides: "So, with all this murder and blinding and cannibalism, I grew up with a concept of drama as something naturally dark and bloody."

As a student, Rudkin did a spell of pear picking in Worcestershire wherein he observed the labourers ragging an Irish labourer. He decided to abandon literary language and write a play from experience – a drama of workaday observation and banter. But he found, as the taunting became crueller, more relentless, that he was being driven across the naturalistic threshold into occultism and sexual deviance – areas that might draw down the wrath of the censor. The finished play was performed by the Royal Shakespeare Company. Set in the Vale of Evesham, it portrays a group of regular pear-pickers ganging up on and ultimately eliminating a fellow worker – an old tramp they call Shakespeare.

The tramp, whose stage name is Roche, calls himself a poet. From time to time, he expresses lofty, anti-materialistic sentiments, shot through with religious allusion. But this does not impress his colleagues. Roche is scapegoated for being lazy and indirectly causing the fall of a woman from a tree he had picked inadequately.

The finale is shocking. The pear-pickers encircle and accuse Shakespeare and, "afore night come", plunge their knives into his body, scoring it with a cross and then spearing the head to the ground by driving a pitchfork through the neck, afterwards beheading and burying it.

Why they sacrifice him in such a blatantly pagan way is none too clear, save there is a sense, as in the Walton Murder, of the antagonists sticking to the tools of their trade. Although Roche was 'an outsider', who had courted controversy, he had done nothing to deserve the fate meted out to him. The final stage directions recall the murder field in Lower Quinton:

Silence. Almost dark now. In distance, rumble of traffic; sound of heavy industry; slight wind again...Stage empty, except for hayfork, standing, prong-fixed in ground, in a pale shaft of moonlight that strays upon it. Wind dies. Noises, then moonlight, fade. Darkness, silence, emptiness.

*Inspector Fabian brooding on the Old Steps at Wapping,
a notorious locale for criminal operations.*

PAUL NEWMAN

Born in Bristol, England, Paul Newman turned to full-time writing in the 1970s, since when he has published various titles on history, symbolism, literature and topography, notably *The Hill of the Dragon* (1979); *Somerset Villages* (1986); *Bath* (1986); *Bristol* (1987); *The Meads of Love* (1994); *Lost Gods of Albion* (1998); *In Many Ways Frogs* (poems with A R Lamb 1997) and *A History of Terror* (2000). Former editor of Abraxas – a journal devoted to literature and ideas – his articles and stories have featured in *Writers Monthly*, *3ʳᵈ Stone*, *South West Arts*, *Westwords*, *Cornish Review*, *Psychopoetica*, *Ramraid Extraordinaire*, *Story Cellar* and *Dreams From A Stranger's Café*. His novel *Galahad* (2003) won the Peninsula Prize and his latest books include *The Tregerthen Horror* (2006), *Ancestral Voices Prophesying War* (2008) and *The Man Who Unleashed the Birds: Frank Baker & his Circle* (2010).

THE MAN WHO UNLEASHED THE BIRDS
Frank Baker & his Circle

In 1963 the world of entertainment was transfixed by the terrifying movie *The Birds* directed by Alfred Hitchcock and based on a short story by Daphne du Maurier. But what many people do not know was that the same story had been written thirty years earlier by a brilliant young writer called Frank Baker who depicted the city of London falling apart as it was mercilessly attacked by a mysterious flock of birds. This novel had been forgotten and Baker was smarting in penury as he watched what he saw as his own creation go on to reap thousands of dollars. Isolated and neglected, bisexual and devoted to alcohol, he felt very much a literary leftover, hiding away with his family mainly in the duchy of Cornwall, about which he wrote with tremendous passion in his brooding, melodramatic first novel *The Twisted Tree* (1935). This pioneering biography tells his story for the first time against the backdrop of the artistic colony in Cornwall before and after World War Two.

166

Galahad by PAUL NEWMAN
Reviewed by Colin Stanley

In a recent survey it was revealed that of all the centuries, the fourteenth century was by far the worst. What with the Hundred Years' War, the Black Death, various social crises and revolts and religious persecution, you were lucky if you survived much of it. The population was decimated by war, disease and famine.

By comparison, the Dark Ages, as described by Paul Newman in this novel, was like a walk in the park. That is, of course, if you survived the floods, the pox, the dragons; and avoided the wrath of the Vikings, being scorched alive in a wicker man and beheaded on the battlefield. All of these our slightly tarnished hero Galahad sidesteps in his quest for the Holy Grail.

Intending, in the opening chapters, to join a monastery, he is diverted on the way by a naked lovely, the sight of which "…stirred me at a most profound level…" All is lost and on the erect phallus of the Cerne Giant he is initiated – the first of many sexual encounters for the hero (well, what else is there to do during those long dark ages?).

The subsequent adventures he describes, and the characters he meets, before his quest comes to an unexpected conclusion, are obviously the products of an unusually witty and surreal mind.

Divided into 20 largely self-contained chapters, each vying to be more bizarre than the others, the mushrooms really start to kick-in around chapter 10 which describes the trial of a mouse accused of theft. Chapter 11 introduces a singing dog whose rendition of *My Dear Old Headhunting Mama* lays a ghostly Druid to rest. And in chapter 12, we meet the awesome Herne the Hunter in Wandlebury Forest, who, wishing to be rid of his horns, has a seemingly unfortunate accident which rids him of his body instead and dooms his head to be dragged across the earth by oxen for all eternity. But fret not…he appears again in a later chapter well pleased with his lot.

A good novel can be gauged, I think, by how quickly you read it, how much valuable time you are willing to sacrifice at each sitting. Even a slow and careful reader like myself was able to breeze through this entertaining tale. It was, no doubt, also a breath of fresh air to the Peninsula Prize judges.

PRESS OPINIONS

The Meads of Love (1994)
The biography, the first since the poet's son wrote an idealised portrait following Harris's death, is written with wit and style; it sets the homespun life against the great events of the time, and uses the poems to make intelligent guesses about Harris's character.

     (DM Thomas – *The Guardian*)

Lost Gods of Albion (1998)
The delight of this book is that it is a well-read and wry survey of the extraordinary variety of response and interpretation the hill-figures have evoked down the centuries.

     (Richard Mabey – *Daily Telegraph*)

The greatest strength of this work is data, the objective information about situation, measurement and known history of each monument, presented fairly and with good humour and a superb garnish of evocative prose. The book is a useful corpus of fact and a fine example of the twentieth-century imagination at work.

     (Ronald Hutton – *Antiquity*)

A History of Terror (2000)
Since human beings became aware of their own existence, people have been afraid. But have they always been afraid of the same things? Wild animals, spirits, demons and psychopaths: down the ages, the objects of our anxieties have changed and shifted. In this elegantly written, engagingly conversational and superbly informative book, Paul Newman charts the shapes and sizes our fear has taken, from the rustic 'panic' of ancient herdsmen suddenly confronted with the Great God of the wild, to postmodern websurfers, overwhelmed by the glut of useless facts on the 'information superhighway'.

     (Gary Lachman – *Fortean Times*)

Galahad (2003)
Brilliant – Galahad lights up the Dark Ages.

     (*Colin Wilson*)

Lightning Source UK Ltd.
Milton Keynes UK
UKOW03f2143160114

224776UK00005B/237/P

9 781898 343127